At-Risk Youth

AT-RISK YOUTH
Identification, Programs, and Recommendations

SHIRLEY E. WELLS

LIBRARY

1990
TEACHER IDEAS PRESS
A Division of
Libraries Unlimited, Inc.
Englewood, Colorado

TEACHER IDEAS PRESS
A Division of
Libraries Unlimited, Inc.
P.O. Box 3988
Englewood, CO 80155-3988

Library of Congress Cataloging-in-Publication Data

Wells, Shirley E.
　　At-risk youth : identification, programs, and recommendations /
Shirley E. Wells.
　　xii, 158 p. 17x25 cm.
　　Includes bibliographical references.
　　ISBN 0-87287-812-0
　　1. Dropouts--Services for--United States. 2. Socially handicapped
youth--Education--United States. 3. Hispanic American youth-
-Education. 4. Dropout behavior, Prediction of. I. Title.
LC146.6.W45　　1990
371.2'913--dc20　　　　　　　　　　　　　　　　90-31098
　　　　　　　　　　　　　　　　　　　　　　　　　CIP

Contents

Preface

This review of research explores five categories of characteristics which student dropouts and potential dropouts tend to exhibit. Certain family, student, school, and community predictors, as well as demographic considerations, tend to indicate variables related to decisions by students to drop out of school. These characteristics can be used as predictors of potential dropouts at early ages. When analyzing characteristic data, however, it is important to review the variables in combination with each other, and not in isolation when determining a student to be "at-risk."

Identification systems are just now beginning to emerge at local school district levels in an attempt to provide a vehicle through which students can be identified for intervention strategies. Districts acknowledge struggling in the development of efficient systems. Many districts have created checklists designed from lists of characteristic indicators to be used by teachers and other school district personnel when identifying students who may be at risk of dropping out of school. Guidance or staff teams consisting of various professionals, parents, and social service agency personnel are utilized by districts to review histories of students who have been identified as potentially at risk. The same team then explores options available to the student as intervention strategies. Some districts and researchers are exploring data analysis options in the early prediction of student dropouts.

Many programs for potential student dropouts, particularly at the secondary level, have existed for several years. Alternative high schools, teen pregnancy programs, and discipline systems, among others, have attempted to address the needs of the student population we are now describing as at risk. The discussion in this report of successful program components and actual program descriptions are useful when developing overall, integrated intervention strategies and systems to address the needs of students who are viewed as potential dropouts. Effective interventions seem to result from a combination of programs, systems, and services, school, community, and parent commitment to success, and the tailoring of needed intervention to individual students. The design of success may be viewed as complex, but it is not impossible.

Recommendations to school districts provide avenues to address needs of at-risk students. The recommendations emerged from a review of research literature and from professionals offering strategies that have worked. Finally, appendixes A and B provide examples of identification checklists of students at risk and program descriptions from all grade levels that exist across the country.

Over four months, I contacted more than 100 school districts and state departments of education, researching current practices with youth at risk while working for the Education Commission of the States. I was gratified to find many "exemplary" programs so designated by state departments, local school districts, and research articles and documents. In addition, many states and local education agencies sent to me descriptions of programs they thought might be worth sharing. The enthusiasm of educators sharing information and asking for additional information in the field was overwhelming. It was truly a networking experience, and one I wanted to share with others. Appendix B has been arranged in six categories: curriculum-related programs including early childhood; alternative programs; student assistance programs, including substance abuse, teen pregnancy, and other health related programs; vocational and work/study programs; family support programs; attendance and truancy prevention programs; and business and community-related programs. For the convenience of the reader, each section begins with elementary level, moves to middle school, and finally to high school and adult-level programs.

Acknowledgments

I'd like to express my appreciation to Adams County School District #50, Colorado and specifically to Dr. Michael Massarotti for his vision in originally asking me to take on the task of researching the information in this book. The Education Commission of the States, Denver, Colorado, was the vital link in connecting me with countless resources around the country and giving me the freedom to gather information useful to us both.

List of Abbreviations

ACCEPT	Alachua County Continuing Education for Pregnant Teens
ACE	Alternative Center for Education
APL	Adult Performance Level
APP	Absentee Prevention Program
BB/BS	Big Brothers/Big Sisters
CARE	Career Awareness Related Education
CARES	Care and Concern Team
CCP	Comprehensive Competencies Program
COFFEE	Cooperative Federation for Educational Experiences
DAP-CEP	Detroit Area Pre-College Engineering Program
EBD	Emotional/Behavioral Disorder
ELC	Early Learning Center
ESL	English as a Second Language
EXPO	Experiential Program for Orientation
FLEC	Family Life Education Center
GED	General Equivalency Diploma
IEP	Individual Education Plan
ILP	Individual Learning Program
INS	Immigration and Naturalization Services
IOU	Individualized Opportunities Unlimited
ISR	Internal Suspension Room

JDRP	Joint Dissemination and Review Panel
JTPA	Job Training Partnership Act
MLC	Metropolitan Learning Center
MOT	Management Outreach Team
NCE	Normal Curve Equivalent
OASIS	Opportunity at Suspension in Schools
PAS	Program Assessment and Support
PASS	Positive Alternatives to Student Suspensions
PHALC	Port Huron Alternative Learning Center
PLL	Prescription Learning Lab
SAE	Screening, Assignment & Evaluation Committee
SAIL	School for Applied Individualized Learning
SLC	Secondary Learning Center
SOS	Students Offering Support
SWOHS	Southwest Open High School
SYETP	Summer Youth Employment and Training Program
TAP	Teenage Parent Program
TLC	Teens Learning to Care
WECEP	Work Experience Career Exploration Program
YDC	Youth Development Center
YEAH	Youth Excited About Helping

Introduction

Students who drop out of school have long been viewed as a problem both educationally and socially. According to the U.S. Bureau of Census (1985), dropout rate history among persons 25 to 29 years of age has decreased substantially over the past 40 years. The dropout rate in 1900 was 94 percent (Orum, 1984), 60 percent in 1940, and 16 percent in 1980 (Rumberger, 1986). According to Orr (1987), dropout rates have remained unchanged for the past 20 years. Minority populations are increasing in public schools, and those students have historically shown higher dropout rates than the white population (Rumberger, 1986). Current legislative efforts to raise academic requirements for high school graduation might have an adverse effect on youth at risk of dropping out (McDill, Natriello, and Pallas, 1985; American Journal of Education, 1986). With increased use of new technologies and changes in the composition of jobs in our economy, educational requirements and skills in the work place are increasing (National Commission of Excellence in Education, 1983; Task Force on Education Economic Growth, 1983).

Increased attention to dropout populations has become a political issue in this nation. Competitive predictors of economic superiority have caused us to look at, among other things, indicators judging the nation's and states' school systems. High school completion rate is one such indicator.

The consequences of dropping out are perhaps the most critical reason for our concern as a nation. Henry M. Levin of Stanford University, in a report prepared for the U.S. Senate Select Committee on Equal Educational Opportunity, concluded that youths failing to complete high school are more likely to become economic burdens to society (Levin, 1972). The economic burden of dropouts is felt in increased taxes to support welfare programs, fight crime, and maintain special programs, as well as in lost revenue through lack of taxes generated by these former students who may not be working or who may be in lower-paying occupations (Catterall, 1985). Further, according to Levin, these youth are less likely to move up the socioeconomic ladder or participate in the decisionmaking processes of government. Dropouts generate considerably less income over their lifetimes than do graduates (Catterall, 1985).

This book is a review of research on youth at risk of dropping out of school. The report includes (1) characteristics of these students, (2) identification systems, (3) characteristics/components of successful programs in addition to actual program descriptions, and (4) recommendations to school districts on developing a district-wide approach to the problems of youth at risk.

Characteristics

In *Reconnecting Youth*, the Education Commission of the States (1985), lists three categories of youth at risk of dropping out: the alienated, the disadvantaged and alienated, and the disadvantaged. The alienated group is identified as those uninterested in or dissatisfied with the values presented by school and work. They come from middle-class, urban, and rural settings. The disadvantaged and alienated exhibit alienation symptoms and lack basic social and academic skills, family support, and self-esteem. The disadvantaged group is defined as those students who have family support and motivation to succeed, but suffer from effects of economic deprivation and racial discrimination.

Most researchers break characteristics of potential dropouts and dropouts into five major categories: family-related; school-related, including cognitive and affective characteristics; student-related; community-related; and demographic. Some characteristics cross categories, while some are seen in isolation or in combinations. We know which characteristics tend to indicate that students may be at risk, but do not at this point have a means to predict with 100 percent accuracy which students will drop out or will complete school. With extensive data collection and analysis, however, we can predict to a higher degree those who may drop out (Brown, 1988). The process of becoming a dropout is complex and long term. Failure of students, families, schools, and society all contribute to the accumulation of concrete problems which eventually result in dropping out.

FAMILY-RELATED CHARACTERISTICS

Data from *High School and Beyond* show that 17 percent of the 1980 high-school sophomore cohort who were from low socioeconomic status (SES) families dropped out, as compared to 9 percent and 5 percent from middle and high SES families (Peng and Takai, 1983). Factors within low SES include low educational and occupational attainment levels of parents, frequent high-school noncompletion rates of one or both parents, low family income, larger family, weak family cohesiveness or single-parent family, and the lack of learning materials and opportunities in the home (Rumberger, 1983; Steinberg, Blinde, and Chan, 1982; Bachman, 1971). A study by the National Association of School Social Workers (NASSW) found that additional family-related barriers to school tend to be child abuse and neglect, divorce and separation, parental apathy, family crisis, and poverty (NASSW, 1985).

Other indicators of family-related characteristics contributing to at-risk status include an excessively stressful home life, poor communication between home and school, racial or ethnic minority, non-English-speaking home, siblings and/or parents who were dropouts, frequent family moves, and changing schools (California State DOE, 1986). Conversely, white and Hispanic, but not black, students who come from intact, two-parent families are less likely to drop out of school, as are students of higher SES (Ekstrom et al., 1986). Children feel insecure when parent/child relationships are disturbed and begin to feel alienated. This can create difficulty in a child's ability to pay attention in school (Bronfenbrenner, 1986).

SCHOOL-RELATED CHARACTERISTICS

Most school-related factors tend to be visible and gain considerable attention, such as acting out. Others are less recognized, such as poor interpersonal relationships, but nonetheless exist and contribute to the dropout problem. Recently, the schools themselves have been considered as influential in students' decisions to drop out.

Two major visible school-related factors are poor academic achievement and behavior problems in school. Poor academic achievement can be measured by grades, test scores, and grade retention (Wehlage and Rutter, 1986). Failure in one or more schools, low math and reading scores, lack of basic skills, and verbal deficiency are further contributing measures (Wisconsin, 1981; California, 1986).

Cognitive characteristics of youth at risk include low average IQ scores, low achievement scores, and high grade retention rates. Dropouts tend to fall in the bottom quartiles on nationally administered reading and math tests (San Diego, 1985). They are generally two or more years behind in reading or math, and basic skills levels are well below average for their grade level (Weber, 1983). The Los Angeles Unified School District (LAUSD, 1985) study found that dropouts are held back five times more often than graduates. LAUSD also found that less proficient students who fail either of the first two grades have only a 20 percent chance of graduating. Additionally, student failure at the eighth or ninth grade is crucial in a student's decision to drop out (LAUSD, 1985). A social psychologist at the University of Pennsylvania (Fine, 1986), states that in her studies of New York City dropouts, being held back in school is the best single predictor of dropping out.

Intelligence and academic ability of dropouts do not appear to be very different from those of students who do graduate but do not attend college. Greater differences in intellectual and academic abilities are evident between college-bound graduates and non-college-bound students (Weber, 1983).

Affective characteristics of students associated with dropping out are feelings of alienation and behavior problems including absenteeism, truancy, and discipline problems (Wehlage and Rutter, 1986). Students who cut classes and are seen by administration for disciplinary problems, have been suspended and/or are in trouble with police, are more likely to drop out (Ekstrom et al., 1986). Most of these discipline problems are visible from elementary school, particularly attendance. Students who are overage tend to display behavior problems and are more likely to drop out (Hammack, 1986). Dropouts report feeling alienated from schools, teachers, peers, homes, neighborhoods, and/or society in general (LAUSD, 1985). They tend to perceive little interest, caring, or acceptance on the part of teachers, and are discouraged by the school's constant signals to them about their academic failures (Wehlage and Rutter, 1986). In addition, dropouts tend to be resentful of authority and feel that the school's discipline system is unfair and ineffective (Wehlage and Rutter, 1986).

Schools themselves may influence students' decisions to dropout, although little attention or concrete evidence has proven this. Dropouts indicate dissatisfaction with school, do not think they can get along with teachers, and report an inability to deal with school structure as reasons for dropping out (Stern, 1986; Rumberger, 1986). Larry Cuban (1989) agrees that the inflexibility of schools and school systems contributes to student academic failure and poor performance. The "graded school," he contends, is one of the most inflexible of the structures. All students are expected to learn and retain information at the same pace or be left behind by their peers. Schools eliminate those who perform or behave in contrast to the norm.

Many potential dropouts do attend schools with very poor facilities, inadequate teaching staffs, and inadequate materials. Such factors could affect their performance in school and their decision to drop out (Fine, 1986). Negative school environment or school climate may contribute to dropping out. The National Association of School Social Workers (NASSW) cited such school-related contributors as lack of positive, cooperative relationships between and among students, staff, parents, and administrators; inadequate discipline procedures and/or policies; lack of alternative schools/programs to meet the needs of at-risk groups; and lack of collaborative teamwork among school and community professionals (NASSW, 1985).

Wehlage and Rutter (1986) stated that in the process of becoming a dropout, the act of rejecting the educational institution must also be accompanied by the belief that the institution has rejected the person. The process is cumulative and begins with negative messages from the school concerning academic or discipline problems. Further, schools may contribute to high dropout rates by treating students as children who have no responsibility (Education Week, 1986; Stern, 1986). Institutions, the Education Week report claims, demand no commitment of students except to their own personal development.

STUDENT-RELATED CHARACTERISTICS

Dropouts have lower levels of self-concept and self-esteem, and indicate that they feel they have less overall control over their lives than do other students (Rumberger, 1986). They exhibit poor attitudes about school and have low educational and occupation aspirations (Ekstrom et al., 1986; Wehlage and Rutter, 1986). Dropouts often exhibit immaturity, frequent health problems, inability to identify with other people, drug and alcohol abuse, pregnancy, lack of motivation, lack of social adjustment, and court-related problems (California, 1986). Dropouts themselves report, in addition to these elements, family problems, work responsibilities, and conflict with other students as reasons for leaving school (LAUSD, 1985).

Lehr and Harris (1988) describe possible characteristics of at-risk students as exhibiting academic difficulties, inattentiveness, short attention span, low self-esteem, excessive absences, perhaps health-related problems, lack of social skills, inability to face pressure, and lack of motivation. Students may be disorganized and need assistance in learning organizational techniques. They also may be very dependent if they have not experienced much success in learning.

Economic factors are reported by dropouts as influential in the decision to leave school. About 20 percent of dropouts reported they left school because they felt they had to help support their families. Many dropouts report leaving school to get married or because they are pregnant (Rumberger, 1983; Ekstrom et al., 1986).

COMMUNITY-RELATED CHARACTERISTICS

Community factors present an equally complex set of characteristics leading to the decision of students eventually to drop out. Barriers include a lack of (1) responsive community support services; (2) linkages between school and community services; (3) preventive mental health programs to address drug and alcohol problems; (4) family counseling; (5) community support for schools; (6) "neighborhood" schools; (7) adequate transportation; and

(8) ability to deal with the high incidence of criminal activity (NASSW, 1985; Pasternak, 1986).

DEMOGRAPHIC CHARACTERISTICS

Demographic data from the *High School and Beyond* study, which are supported by other studies, indicate that dropout rates for males and females were similar for the 1980 high school sophomores studied (U.S. Census, 1985; LAUSD, 1985; San Diego City Schools, 1985). Fourteen percent left school during or after their sophomore year and before completing graduation requirements. Of that group, 24 percent left in the 10th grade, 47 percent in the 11th grade, and 29 percent of the 12th grade.

Dropout rates among racial/ethnic groups differ. Recent short-term increases in dropouts have been seen among white students, while black students—who still drop out in higher numbers than white students—have shown a decline in dropout rates since 1970 (*Reconnecting Youth*, ECS, 1985). Hispanic students have a generally increasing dropout rate which is higher than the overall national figures: 30 percent in 1974, 40 percent in 1979, and 45 percent in 1984 (Steinberg, Blinde, and Chan, 1982). Almost 40 percent of Hispanic males reported dropping out for economic reasons such as home responsibilities, financial difficulties, and good job offers (Rumberger, 1983).

Characteristics of Hispanic
Students at Risk

Common characteristics of all dropouts, with the possible exception of language, seem to be consistent regardless of ethnic background. However, particularly high numbers of dropouts among Hispanics and perhaps some cultural differences stimulate interest in examining the Hispanic student group. Hispanic students represent the highest dropout group of all ethnic groups.

Family background and responsibilities, parental expectations, and school experiences affect all students throughout their schooling. Hispanic students are the most undereducated group of Americans and have been characterized by below-grade-level enrollment, high rates of illiteracy, and low number of school years completed (Orum, 1986). Those students who are significantly older than their class peers tend to experience discipline problems, boredom, and low self-esteem. School successes or failures beginning in the elementary grades tend to influence students' self-perceptions of their ability to complete school, and contribute to feelings of alienation or belonging (Orum, 1984).

A series of articles in the *Rocky Mountain News* (Denver, Colorado) reported several experiences of Hispanic students, both culturally and in school, that contribute to dropping out. Traditionally, for Hispanics, learning takes place verbally, through storytelling, apprenticeship, and experiences. Reading, then, is a different learning experience. Schools tend to be competitive, whereas the Hispanic culture is cooperative. Hispanic students, according to sociologists, tend to lose self-esteem when they sense that teachers expect them to fail, and counselors do not push them into academic courses or encourage them to go to college (Enda, 1986).

Beyond Language reported three possible differences between particular cultures which might lead to more dropping out among some groups, including Hispanics. Cultures which were incorporated by conquest (in this case blacks and Hispanics) tend to not fare as well educationally as those who have chosen to immigrate (Orientals). Oral language skills are predominant among Hispanic families. Adults often do not talk directly to children, nor do children traditionally participate in family communication until they are older. Cooperative, not competitive, family values are common among Hispanic families, while competition is a highly respected value among Oriental families (*Beyond Language*, 1986). Since the school culture relies on direct communication and encourages competition, Hispanic students may find themselves at a disadvantage in school.

Research tends to identify some school-related factors as variables which can intensify the predisposition of Hispanic students toward dropping out. "Students placed in remedial instructional tracks are more likely to encounter low teacher expectations of academic success" (Phelan and Gibson, 1986). Negative peer friendships (that is, friendships with the "wrong" kind of kids) emerge among similarly placed students in low academic tracks. Further, these students tend not to participate in extracurricular activities.

Studies have indicated common factors of potential Hispanic dropouts, which have been further broken into two categories: personal and school characteristics. *Personal characteristics* include high absenteeism, lack of academic success, repeated suspensions, low parent involvement, teenage pregnancy, economically disadvantaged background, single parent family, and low self-esteem. *School factors* include lack of Hispanic role models among teachers and other school staff, lack of support from school counselors, lack of language program needs, high pupil/teacher ratios, and limited resources (Orum, 1984; Rodriquez, 1985).

Additional factors seem to be consistent with overall dropout characteristics. Some of these include being overage for their grade, frequent discipline problems, boredom, and poor self-image. Hispanics tend to have low enrollment in work-study and cooperative education programs. One reason for low enrollment is that participation often requires a specific grade-point average (Orum, 1984).

Lack of parental involvement in the schools is a problem particularly among Hispanic families. Hispanic students in predominantly Spanish-speaking homes may feel a strong of cultural pressure to maintain Spanish language usage (Steinberg, Blinde, and Chan, 1982). Language problems can become a critical barrier to school completion. Premature school exiting is more common among students who are not English-speaking, or are limited English-speaking. Three factors contribute to a greater school-leaving tendency among language-minority students: (1) early academic failure; (2) more negative interaction with teachers and school personnel; and (3) a gap between language-minority youth needs and school programs (Steinberg et al., 1982).

AT-RISK STUDENT PROFILE

The following At-Risk Student Profile is an attempt to give an overview of student characteristics that often result in the decision to leave school. It must be noted that the interlocking grouped predictors are a necessary component of the overall picture, with some exceptions such as pregnancy. Many single characteristics do not necessarily result in students leaving school; however, combinations from the various groups can indicate the at-risk status of individual students. In the identification portion of this report, examples are given of particular variables which tend to be higher predictors of at-risk students in general and which are more commonly investigated by educators. Table 1, page 10, demonstrates Student Profile Characteristics grouped into four categories.

In summary, there tend to be common predictors which vary from group to group in frequency, but nevertheless identify students at risk of dropping out of school. Characteristics of students who have already dropped out seem to be useful as predictors of potential dropouts at earlier grade levels. It is important to note that characteristic indicators must be viewed in combination and not in isolation when determining a student to be at-risk. A specific characteristic may not lead to actually dropping out. *Sets* of characteristics, however, appear to be more substantial indicators when determining the potential for dropping out.

Table 1
At-Risk Student Profile Characteristics

School-Related

- Low teacher expectations
- Lack of language instruction
- Conflict between home/school culture
- Overcrowded classrooms
- Lack of adequate counseling
- Counseling referrals
- Poor facilities
- Lack of educational options/inadequate curriculum
- Negative school environment, climate
- Lack of adequate attendance system
- Lack of adequate discipline system
- Institutional discrimination
- Higher graduation requirements
- Retention
- Suspensions
- Special program placement
- Placement in tracks other than high academics
- Low ability level
- Low grade-point average
- Low standardized test, reading, math and composite scores

Community-Related

- Lack of community support services or response (drug & alcohol abuse programs, family counseling, mental health & social services)
- Lack of community support for schools
- High incidences of criminal activities—poor response from court system
- Lack of school community linkages
- Loss of neighborhood schools

Wells and Bechard, 1989

Student-Related

- Poor school attitudes
- Low motivation
- Low education and occupational aspirations
- Attendance/truancy problems
- Low self-esteem, external locus of control
- Behavior/discipline problems
- Pregnancy, marriage
- Drug abuse
- Poor peer relationships
- Nonparticipation in extracurricular activities
- Negative police involvement
- Lack of student responsibility
- Friends have dropped out
- Illness and disability

Family-Related

- Low SES (free/reduced lunch)
- Student has to work
- Stressful homelife (dysfunctional)
- Parental noninvolvement (low expectation)
- Low parental education level and occupation
- Non-English-speaking home (excluding Asian)
- Abuse
- Ineffective parenting
- Number of school moves
- Minority status

SYMPTOMS IN
COMBINATION INCREASE
RISK

Identification Systems for At-Risk Students

NEED FOR IDENTIFICATION SYSTEMS

Research indicates that the act of dropping out is the end result of a process that has taken place over time. While many states and local school districts have developed programs to prevent students from dropping out, most have not looked at a systematic process with which to identify those students. The weakest link has been in the area of identifying students in early grades, which could allow educators to institute appropriate early intervention strategies for students at risk of dropping out. Early intervention is recognized as crucial to limiting the perpetuation of students at risk in later years. A system does not yet exist, in most districts, to identify and track these students across grades or across schools so that school professionals have access to accurate data on students who merit special attention (Mizell, 1986). The national longitudinal study, *High School and Beyond* (Peng and Takai, 1983), assisted the educational community by identifying significant variables among school dropouts. Those variables can be a basis for developing a locally based instrument and process for early identification of potential dropouts.

SUGGESTIONS AND CAUTIONS

A variety of approaches to the identification of at-risk students is essential for early intervention. The National Foundation for the Improvement of Education suggests five keys to the identification process in *Operation Rescue: A*

Blueprint for Success. (1) Teachers should be involved as members of the team identifying students who are at risk. (2) Look at the total school population when identifying students at risk. (3) Use objective data but do not be bound by it; beware of inaccurate data. (4) Find creative ways to identify at-risk students—use subjective means. (5) Look for the invisible dropouts, those whose imaginations have dropped out though their bodies are present (*Operation Rescue*, 1986).

Florida Atlantic University (*Dropout Prevention*, 1986), in an attempt to develop and validate a potential dropout profile for Florida school districts, made the following observations:

1. Identification studies frequently use data not readily available in student records (e.g., views, observations, and peer tracking).

2. Some identification systems use only recent variables prior to student dropout rather than long-range factors.

3. Profiles that consist of a list of variables or criteria often do not provide adequate direction to the practitioner because they do not:

   a. identify which are the most important factors

   b. account for certain combinations of variables that may be predictive of a school dropout

   c. identify the critical times at which certain events must occur

   d. adequately define the variables on the list.

4. Identification systems may not be related to available interventions. Many systems or profiles contain a wide variety of factors that are not addressed by existing dropout prevention programs in the district.

5. Although variables such as socioeconomic status, sex, and racial/ethnic group often have predictive power, these are of extremely limited value when the majority of a school's student population is associated with these variables.

6. Many profiles view dropping out as caused by student problems and do not take into account system or school problems.

IDENTIFICATION APPROACHES FOUND IN LITERATURE REVIEW

Many state and local agencies have developed instruments using characteristic indicators of students who have dropped out in the past as tools for identifying at-risk students presently in school. These indicators have been included in checklist forms which are filled out by a variety of people associated with the student.

Some agencies have developed computer-based prediction or identification formulas based on local district research as well as national research. Using descriptive and discriminant analyses based on local data, districts attempt to design identification formulas that can be used in early grades. Both instruments and identification formulas are discussed in the following pages.

Instruments

The *California Curriculum News Report*, October, 1986, ran a "Checklist for Identifying the Potential Dropout" (appendix A). The checklist identifies at-risk factors and relates them to vulnerability to dropping out or completing school. Some of the 19 factors include age, health, family background, attendance, grades, retention, reading ability, social interaction, and motivation. The "ability to read" factor, for example, if found to be two or more years below grade level for an individual student, is marked under the column "Vulnerable to Dropping Out." If the student is at or above grade level, he or she would be marked under the column "Favorable to Completing School."

The **Los Angeles** County Board of Education produced a handbook in 1986 entitled *The Prevention of Truancy: Programs and Strategies That Address the Problems of Truancy and Dropouts*. It is a comprehensive handbook, including step-by-step "how to's" in addressing at-risk populations. Using the handbook as a basis, many California school districts have utilized staff inservice time to develop a system of identification which can lead to appropriate services for students.

The handbook suggests three checklists to be used by school districts to help schools and teachers identify students in need of intervention. "What Is Your School Climate?" is a checklist pertaining to the schools' contribution to positive climate for students. "How Much Do You Know about Your Pupils?" is a general checklist of characteristics that describe high-risk students in the district. "Early Identification of a Potential Dropout" is an individual, teacher-oriented, student checklist describing nonschool, school-related, and family-related factors (appendix A). Districts using the handbook have also provided staff inservices on how to identify the at-risk pupil by identifying factors such as nonattendance, school climate improvement, and parent and community involvement systems.

Downey Unified School District in Los Angeles County, California, used a referral system along with the checklists described in the Los Angeles handbook. Students are referred by themselves, teachers, parents, or administrators to the school counselor, who then refers the student to a "guidance team." The team, which operates like a special education staffing team, reviews the referral to determine if the student should be identified as being at risk of dropping out. If the student is determined to be at risk, he or she is then referred to appropriate programs and services.

Oakland County in **Pontiac, Michigan,** has developed a series of informational books to assist local districts' dropout prevention efforts. The County Office of Oakland Schools conducted a survey in 1985 as a research base for identifying potential dropouts at the earliest possible grade level. After a review of the literature, the county used 17 factors on the survey of common characteristics of students that drop out. Local school districts then used similar factors to identify students at risk for placement or services (appendix A). Some factors in the "Dropout Identification Survey" include: grade failure, financial need, marriage, school discipline, poor attendance, language difficulty, home stress, poor self-concept, dislike for school, and frequent moves. The survey further indicates, in the opinion of the teacher, whether the factor is one that is controlled or caused by the school, home, or community environments.

A local school district, Granville, in **North Carolina,** developed an early identification referral form to be used by individual school districts in the identification of potential dropouts. Granville uses the form as a referral process by the classroom teacher, counselor, administrator, or parents. The information is sent to the state office as well as the students' records. Counselors are then responsible for placing students into appropriate programs and/or services. The referral form includes two major sections: Factual Characteristics, including attendance, school grade retention, basic skills, subjects failed, and family history; and Observable Characteristics, including school performance, behavior, study/work habits, participation in extracurricular and other activities, self-concept, and personal characteristics, such as types of friends, substance abuse, physical and/or mental health problems (appendix A). Staff development has been implemented to further enhance the process.

Dade County School District in **Miami, Florida,** developed a profile to identify potential dropouts. The central administration compiles student information into the central computer system and then generates a list of each schools' potential dropouts. The potential dropout profile is used as a probability indicator and as an identification/counseling tool. Profile variables include:

- Major exceptionality (student in special education or Chapter 1 program)

- Limited English proficiency

- 18 or more absences per year

- Two or more years older than the average age for the grade level

- Reading stanine less than 4

- Attended three or more schools

- Three or more Ds or Fs for the most current grading period

- Total days of indoor or outdoor suspension in one school year

- Severity (matches two or more of the profile criteria).

Another profile was developed by the **Panhandle Area Education Cooperative (PAEC), Florida**. Characteristics of actual dropouts were identified by guidance counselors, and the most common characteristics were compiled into a list. A computer database was developed which included a record system of all students, kindergarten through grade 12. The records include potential dropout identifiers that become part of a student's permanent file. A report is compiled by PAEC and given to school guidance counselors, who in turn help plan appropriate intervention/prevention programs (*Dropout Prevention* handbook, 1986). Characteristics used include academic achievement, attendance, behavior referrals, pregnancy, economic pressures (family's or student's), and any linkages with other social agencies.

Denver, Colorado, uses school-related factors to identify potential dropouts. School variables, which include poor academic achievement, poor attendance, behavior problems, and repeating grades, are used because they can be measured objectively and are readily available in a school system. Four specific predictor variables are identified: grade point average, percent absence, number of suspensions, and competency test scores in reading, mathematics, language usage, and spelling. A computer program is utilized which includes the four specific predictor variables along with school achievement variables (grade point average, special education, days absent in present semester, days suspended, number of suspensions, and standardized test scores) as well as demographic data (name, age, sex, and racial or ethnic group). These reports are then sent to the school counselors on request so that attention and/or special programs can be provided to these students.

Local Data Analyses

Edmonds School District, Washington, using a locally adapted version of the *High School and Beyond* survey, surveyed student attitudes of high school freshmen and followed them through their high school careers as part of a longitudinal study which began in 1983. A predictor formula was developed from survey and student records data which allowed the district to identify potential dropouts and graduates. Results indicated a fairly accurate predictor model. Variables emerged which distinguished between eventual dropout and graduate groups, and showed which are under the control of the school. Significant distinguishing variables were academic history, behavior, educational expectations, attitude toward school, school qualities, and how time is spent outside of school (Brown, 1988).

Highlands County School District, Florida, developed a model used for predicting dropouts based on a study which began in the spring of 1986. Data obtained from student records provided a profile of local dropouts as well as characteristics that differentiated dropouts from completers. Descriptive analysis calculated dropout rates, dropout profiles, and a prediction model for identifying potential dropouts. A regression analysis revealed variables which best differentiated between graduates and dropouts. Those variables include grade point averages, socioeconomic status, number of discipline referrals, basic skills achievement, attendance, and remedial education. Discriminant analyses were also used to provide each student with a probability of being a dropout. Five variables were found to be significant in the discriminant analysis: gender, race, attendance in sixth grade, grade point average in sixth grade, and the SSAT math score (Berquist and Kruppenback, 1987).

Identification criteria tend to use profiles of students taken from characteristics of the dropout population in the research, and/or analysis of localized variables derived through (1) student attitude surveys, (2) school records and student data, (3) exit interviews of dropouts, and/or (4) perceptions of professionals working with students. In some cases, districts have gone further in analyzing variables for weighted significance, and designing formulas through discriminant and factor analyses which can then be applied to similar characteristics exhibited by students in early grades, in an effort to identify early those who might need intervention.

It is important to note that, while checklists are a good beginning to the identification process, they may not be relied upon for prediction of future dropping out or graduating. A student profile may indicate many variables related to dropping out and that student may indeed eventually drop out. However, another student with as many outstanding variables, but perhaps a different set of variables, may not drop out. For example:

Student A (actual case) exhibited the following:

Family Characteristics—low SES, low parental expectations, parental noninvolvement; Student Characteristics—low motivation, low education/occupational aspirations, poor academic achievement, grade retention; School Characteristics—low teacher expectations, overcrowded classrooms, lack of adequate counseling.

This student dropped out of school.

Student B (actual case) exhibited the following:

Family Characteristics—middle to upper SES, single parent family, stressful homelife, high family expectations, high parental education; Student Characteristics—low self-esteem, low reading, poor academic achievement, high ability level, behavior problems, high education/occupational aspirations, nonparticipation in extracurricular activities; School Characteristics—high teacher expectations.

This student graduated and eventually completed a doctoral program.

What seems to make some difference in students' decisions to drop out when considering individual data on students? What factors are more common among those who do drop out of school? Are those factors common to all school districts?

In a paper entitled "How to Identify At-Risk Students," Wells, Bechard, and Hamby (1989) found that effective identification is a process involving a variety of data-collection procedures and analysis, not simply an instrument. When developing a local identification system, they suggest, the more data available, the better the chance of identifying variables that can be good predictors in early grades for students who are developing patterns toward dropping out of school later. The "process" is likened to a jigsaw puzzle in which every piece of data gathered and analyzed gives a clearer, more accurate picture.

A locally developed identification system will be more precise and effective because it will include only those characteristics specific to local populations. The process includes: data collection (checklists, student records data, attitude surveys, exit interviews, etc.), data analysis, data utilization, and design of intervention strategies. The authors detail strategies and recommendations for districts in developing identification systems which will result in strategic intervention programs or strategies (Wells, Bechard, and Hamby, 1989).

SUMMARY

Some consistent threads emerge from the review of identification systems. Most districts are just beginning to design systems to identify students who may be at risk. Identification criteria have up until now tended to use profiles of students taken from characteristics of the dropout population, combined with particular localized characteristics. Local development of identification is a crucial part of the process. With limited dollar resources in education, a more cost-efficient method of identifying students and providing targeted intervention is important. Evaluation of programs and intervention strategies can be tied to the identification process as districts take on the task of designing local identification systems.

Programs
for
At-Risk Students

Programs for dropouts over the years have primarily consisted of alternative schools at the secondary level. Further attention to students exhibiting truant or dropout behavior has often been in the form of discipline, which sometimes results in suspension. A renewed desire to retain students in the school system has caused districts across the country to develop programs to meet the needs of students identified as being at risk of dropping out of school at all levels. Particular attention is now being directed to early identification and prevention in addition to intervention and retrieval programs. Further, the business and community sectors have begun involvement with the schools to address the dropout problem, especially as it relates to the workforce.

One significant finding that has emerged from research on dropouts is the importance of early identification in order to effectively design prevention and intervention programs and strategies. Since students drop out for many reasons, the structure of programs must be responsive to identified personal and environmental needs of those identified as at risk. In order for students to be properly served by prevention or intervention strategies, accurate and objective identification procedures must be used. We can no longer afford the luxury of costly programs without knowing that students being assigned are truly in need of the intervention and that the intervention is effective.

A review of literature suggests many characteristics or elements of successful programs for students who are potential dropouts. While reviewing the research, common program elements emerge. The following discussion reviews general program information and successful program characteristics, with a discussion of program strategies that are effective for Hispanic students. Specific program descriptions from across the country can then be found in appendix B.

GENERAL PROGRAM DISCUSSION

School reform issues surfacing in 1983 and again in 1985 raised significant questions about education in general. However, the at-risk population was not specifically considered during the early reform discussions. Political awareness and concern were raised over the obvious absence of at-risk consideration in the reform reports. Many program-related topics have surfaced throughout the discussion of how to meet the needs of potential dropouts. Effective schools research, restructuring schools, alternative education (kindergarten through grade 12), schools of choice, early childhood education, networking and collaborations with businesses and social agencies, and effective retrieval programs such as adult education, computer-assisted instruction, and work study all play significant roles in looking at and designing "effective" programs that are successful with students identified as being at risk. We know students' learning styles vary, but in conventional schools we often continue to attempt to educate all students in the same manner, without addressing individual needs.

One program or one intervention strategy identified for a student may not be the total answer. Just as the process of dropping out and identifying those who may drop out is complex, so is the development of strategies and programs to meet students' individual needs. Further, program evaluation is critical to assess the impact programs have on students. The following program characteristics, models, cautions, and research should be helpful when considering program design.

Successful Program Characteristics

The California handbook (Los Angeles County, California, 1986), suggests that schools experiencing success in crime and truancy reduction have common threads. Successful schools believe that students can learn and teachers can teach. This is expressed in high academic expectations from everyone. Instructional quality springs from teachers' use of their expertise to find successful teaching strategies. Positive attitudes and respect for students permeate the learning environment, pupils are not ridiculed or ignored, and a strong sense of community and ownership are all predictors of success in at-risk programs. The handbook begins with the premise that school climate and attendance are the keys to the success of students at risk of dropping out.

David Stern (1986) suggests a useful model for dropout prevention programs, noting that there are many different reasons why students drop out of school and that students therefore react differently to programs. Stern recommends categorizing elements of programs into six areas:

1. Curriculum and objective elements—regular, remedial, vocational, specialized, degree-oriented, degree-equivalent-oriented, job-placement-oriented.

2. Location/auspices elements—regular schools, off campus, non-school.

3. Instructional process elements—transforming social relationships, individualization, learning contracts, and group instruction.

4. Staff elements—teachers, counselors, therapists.

5. Related activities elements—counseling, work, community service.

6. Schedule elements—full-time, part-time, short-term, long-term.

Lehr and Harris, in their book *At-Risk, Low-Achieving Students in the Classroom* (1988), describe characteristics of successful student learning. The learning environment should be organized considering: effective schools research, the role of the principal, teacher expectations, grouping students, positive climate, collegial learning, positive discipline, and cooperative learning. Students should be involved in their learning. Successful elements include: (1) instructional processes such as study skills, learning teams, and mnemonic devices; (2) keeping the learner involved with technology, educational games, and simulations, and the newspaper; (3) evaluating the learner's success through various means; and (4) motivational strategies such as supportive environment, appropriate level of challenge/difficulty, programming for success, and allowing choices (Brophy, 1987).

According to Lehr and Harris, classroom teachers get positive results when they attempt to work with the "total child," assisting in the development of that child into a productive member of society. Of the program components described by these authors, teachers' expectations appear to be most critical. Some examples given that communicate "inappropriate" expectations are: seating the student farther away from teacher, giving less direct instruction, asking the student to do less work, calling on the student less often, giving less praise, and criticizing more frequently.

Practitioners acknowledge that programs already in operation in many school districts have been serving most students whom we now categorize as being at risk of dropping out. Many of these same students have been identified in the past through criteria in educational programs such as federal Chapter 1 for the disadvantaged (PL 100-297), Headstart, and special education (PL 94-142). Chapter 1 projects have identified a variety of attributes for success with students (U.S. DOE Sourcebook, 1986). Seven typical examples are:

1. Frequent unit tests to ensure appropriate placement and mastery of learning objectives.

2. Division of learning activities into small units, focusing on one or two skills at a time, allowing students to experience success each day.

3. Provision of individualized study skill activities based on the material introduced and explained in program activities.

4. Cross-age tutoring, with intermediate-level tutors receiving training and ongoing supervision as they work with primary children.

5. Combination of pull-out and in-class instruction.

6. Direct instruction techniques which emphasize clear instructions and reteaching as needed, providing for independent practice and maximizing teacher-student interactions.

7. Computer-assisted instruction to reinforce skills, allowing for individual pacing, and enhancing student motivation.

Effective schools research is important to the success of all students, especially those at-risk. Certain characteristics are common in effective schools (Lehr and Harris, 1988):

- Vigorous instructional leadership
- A principal who makes clear, consistent, and fair decisions
- Emphasis on discipline and a safe and orderly environment
- Instructional practices that emphasize basic skills and academic achievement
- Collegiality among teachers in support of student achievement
- Teachers with high expectations that all students can and will learn
- Frequent review of student progress.

A significant longitudinal study of the effects of the Perry Preschool Program on youth through age 19 was conducted by David Weikart of the High/Scope Educational Research Foundation (Weikart et al., 1984). The study found that early education results in increased academic achievement, as measured by standardized tests, throughout elementary and middle school grades. Children's social and emotional maturity levels were higher. Children were less likely to be placed into special education classes. Fewer absences were noted along with a high value on schooling and a stronger commitment to school. Through secondary school, youth had fewer failing grades and better marks than the control group who did not receive preschool experience. The students as a group spent fewer years in special education and tended instead to be assigned to remedial classes as necessary. At age 19, the preschool group showed higher scores and more favorable attitudes toward school than the non-preschool group. Early education participants were noted to have higher levels of employment, less unemployment, and higher earnings by age 19. Further, members of this group were more likely to be supporting themselves, and were receiving less public assistance than the non-preschool education group. Fewer preschool group subjects had ever been arrested, and fewer pregnancies and births were reported for this group.

Stanford University researcher Henry Levin is developing an "accelerated school" for disadvantaged students in three California school districts. The planning stage of the project began in 1986, with staff from the three districts volunteering for participation. The goal of the project is to eliminate educational disadvantage and remediation by effectively closing the achievement gap by the end of the sixth grade. All students and families must choose to participate; they are not arbitrarily assigned to the accelerated schools. Parents and parent-surrogates must agree to stress the goals of the school, support, encourage, and monitor their child's progress, and provide a place, time, and reinforcement for homework. Where parents cannot provide all of the supports, they must be willing to allow community or other volunteers to take over the responsibilities. No particular method of instruction will be prescribed; however, technical assistance will be provided in designing appropriate programs. The schools began operating in the 1987-1988 school year.

Wehlage, Rutter, and Turnbaugh (1987), describe a "Model Program" that schools can use to retain at-risk high school students. Four categories describe this program:

1. Administration and organization: alternative programs such as schools-within-a-school or independent alternatives, and more personal small programs.

2. Teacher culture: teachers take on an extended role in order to deal with the "whole child" considering with problems in the home, community, or peer group.

3. Student culture: the program is voluntary and students must apply, requires commitment of students, includes peer-monitored behavior, stresses "family" atmosphere.

4. Curriculum: individualized, clear objectives, prompt feedback, and an active role for students. Experiential learning is an important feature of this model providing for improved social skills, social experiences, and development of responsibility.

Alternative education programs, according to Gary Wehlage of the University of Wisconsin/Madison, are among the most successful methods of dealing with secondary at-risk students. Wehlage found six characteristics of successful alternative programs including: (1) small size, (2) program autonomy, independent of traditional programs, (3) a committed teaching force, (4) nontraditional curriculum which includes an individualized approach, cooperative learning, beginning at the individual's level, and use of "real life" examples, (5) experiential education (programs linked to the external community such as work-study, tutoring younger students, and community projects), and (6) positive atmosphere and supportive peer culture (*School Dropouts*, IEL, 1986; Wehlage and Rutter, 1986).

Common components of schools or programs that are successful, according to Larry Cuban of Stanford University, are: (1) small size, (2) staff who have volunteered for the program, (3) flexibility, and (4) classrooms which are communities or family-oriented. Other common characteristics include instructional approaches that build on the strengths of students, learning that connects with the life experiences of students, the development of students' reasoning skills, using mixed-ability and mixed-age groupings within and across classrooms, nongraded classes, and cooperative learning (Cuban, 1989).

Local vocational programs seem to be working to retain students who otherwise might drop out. James Weber, in his publication for the National Center for Research in Vocational Education (1986), describes features of exemplary dropout prevention programs. Common features are classified into three areas: General Organization, Staffing, and Curriculum and Instruction. General Organization features programs in nonconventional school environments, within or outside a conventional school plant. They typically have low teacher-pupil ratios, function somewhat autonomously, and tend to be both holistic and multifaceted in their approaches (remedial basic skills instruction, parental involvement, work experience/job placement, counseling, supportive services, and skill training). Staffing components involve "special" staff and teachers who are committed to the philosophy and goals of the program. These individuals develop close workable relationships with their students and are flexible in their approaches. Curriculum and Instruction efforts address and resolve students' education and remediation needs, personal needs (e.g., self-concept and sense of worth), and work-related needs.

Youth at risk present special problems to employers and potential employers. In *Reconnecting Youth*, the Education Commission of the States

(ECS) challenges private sector colleagues in small and large businesses and in labor to get involved with programs for youth at risk. The Commission further states that many youth can be productive citizens given the right circumstances. Business, it was suggested, should join in cooperative education programs, such as "mentor" programs that link students to particular businesses or trades over months or years. Employers can develop incentives for employees to stay in school, go back to school, or go on to further schooling. Networking with public and private organizations can be beneficial, particularly in training at-risk youth for specific jobs. Small businesses can network with one another to accomplish the same objectives. Businesses and organizations can provide opportunities for employees to work with schools and programs to turn around students at risk. Business advisory councils, roundtables, and other forums can be established with school districts for discourse on public policy issues. Business involvement does make a difference in the issue of youth at risk (ECS, 1985).

The Grant Commission, in its report *The Forgotten Half* (William T. Grant Foundation, 1988), reviewed research and initiatives for non-college-bound students thought to be at risk. They found that all young people need more constructive contact with adults, opportunities to participate in community activities, jobs that offer accomplishment and career opportunity, and special help with difficulties such as learning disabilities and substance addiction. In community-based activities, students should be involved in local governance such as school boards or other governmental and private-sector advisory boards, local crime prevention and neighborhood clean-ups, and law-related activities. Service opportunities offer students the chance to contribute to various community endeavors, both private and public. Among youth community opportunities are Vista, Peace Corps, and the Youth Conservation Corps. Coordinated community services and youth organizations are other areas for youth involvement.

A review of "second chance" programs (Hahn, 1987) revealed the importance of integrating and relating various program or strategy components in a comprehensive effort. Hahn pointed out several important lessons to be learned in designing programs for retrieval and intervention:

1. Isolated work experience is of limited value unless the worksite experience is reinforced in classroom activities clearly connected to the job.

2. Curriculum should relate to the "functional" skills of the workplace.

3. Students should learn to read before they acquire vocational skills.

4. The learning environment should *not* resemble a conventional classroom.

5. Caring teachers, the individuality of students, and teaching technology are important.

6. Students should learn pre-employment and job-related activities such as interviews, writing resumes, and exit interviews.

7. Program services must provide for intensive time on each task.

The misconception that "schools do not cause dropouts and can do nothing to keep children from dropping out" seems to be the most inaccurate belief educators may have about dropouts (Hamby, 1989). John Hamby of the National Dropout Prevention Center describes *awareness*, *attendance*, *achievement*, *attitude*, *atmosphere*, *adaptation*, *alternatives*, and *advocacy* as target areas where schools can make a difference with the at-risk population. He further suggests that the coordinated efforts of all areas of society are needed to solve the problem.

Table 2 lists characteristics of successful programs compiled from sources including the University of Wisconsin Center for Educational Research, the National Association of School Social Workers, the Business Advisory Commission of the Education Commission of the States, the Study Commission on the Quality of Education in the Metropolitan Milwaukee Public Schools, *Effective Compensatory Education Sourcebook*, U.S. Department of Education, University of Miami Center for Dropout Prevention, National Council of La Raza, The Grant Foundation Commission on Work, Family and Citizenship, and various researchers cited in the bibliography.

Table 2

Characteristics of Overall Successful At-Risk Programs

- Preschool early childhood intervention programs
- Small classes
- Program flexibility
- Experience-Based education
- Improved curriculum and improved school climate
- Functional and academically challenging curriculum
- Study skills at all levels
- Self-concept development, student empowerment
- Counseling
- Systematic attendance procedures
- Defined discipline procedure
- Peer tutoring

(Table 2 continues on page 26.)

Table 2 (*continued*)

- Mentor programs
- Interpersonal and life skills
- Systems to address "transition" from home, school, grade level, and beyond
- Vocational/technical/adult education programs
- Work/study programs
- Work attitudes and habits
- School-directed alternative educational programs
- Staff development to better teach all at-risk children, including cultural sensitivity
- High student expectations by teachers
- Hispanic role models in the classroom (teachers, counselors, business, and community leaders)
- Parental involvement
- Student access to schools of their choice
- Student assistance programs to address substance abuse, teen pregnancy and young parenthood, suicide prevention, and other mental and physical health issues, health centers
- Quality after-school care and/or extended day programs
- School-community partnerships
- Business partnerships that smooth the school-to-work transition
- Business incentives to student employees to stay in school
- Community-based youth activities, community service

Hispanic Students

Hispanic students tend to respond to several specific program characteristics. In particular, the literature refers to small classes and personal interaction with Hispanic students as primary interventions. Cooperative learning methods can be highly successful, including cooperative projects for which students share the same grade to cooperative interaction where students take responsibility for specific parts of a project (*Beyond Language*, 1986). High student expectations provide a caring environment, as does peer tutoring and mentor programs (Orum, 1984; Steinberg, Blinde, and Chan, 1982). Personal home contacts appear to be very effective, as are student assistance programs including health care. Counseling, study skills development, and Hispanic role models in the classroom are effective and necessary program components. Work/study opportunities and vocational training can begin to address the family work concern. It must be noted that work/study and vocational training should not take a front seat to basic education skills and enrichment classes that could promote further educational opportunities and future success. These programs can work in harmony to provide the best educational experience for students.

Overall, effective programs for Hispanic students, as well as all at-risk students, result from a combination of programs, components, interaction of school and community personnel, and a desire on the part of district administrators and teachers to succeed with this population. Potential dropouts benefit most from a caring, focused school system that expects and desires students to succeed and is willing to explore all possibilities to bring this desire to fruition.

SUMMARY

Just as student identification is a crucial component to building effective programs and strategies to address needs of students who may be at risk, so is a holistic program approach. Many researchers, commissions, state departments, and private agencies offer a wealth of information regarding the design of successful programs. The research reviewed here is indicative of the information available and should offer practitioners adequate tools with which to design local and student-based programs and strategies.

The specific program descriptions for at-risk youth in appendix B have been divided into seven categories, each beginning with elementary level programs, followed by middle school programs and finally high school programs. The seven categories include: (1) Curriculum-related programs, including early childhood programs; (2) Alternative programs; (3) Student assistance programs, including substance abuse, pregnant teen, suicide prevention, and other health-related programs; (4) Family support programs; (5) Vocational and work/study programs; (6) Attendance and truancy prevention programs; and (7) Business- and community-related programs. Noted for the reader's convenience are program sources and contact persons.

Recommendations to School Districts

The body of this book offers many ideas for the construction of programs and services to meet the needs of at-risk students. A discussion of successful program components provides a starting point in reviewing specific programs, practices, and strategies in use across the country.

Dropout prevention recommendations are suggested in this section. The strategies are research- and practice-based. They are not in a prioritized order, nor are they exhaustive of techniques or strategies available. For ease of use, the recommendations have been grouped into six areas and arranged separately. The six areas are: administrative, curriculum, teacher, school, parent, and work-related strategies.

RECOMMENDATIONS FOR ADMINISTRATORS

- Build dropout prevention efforts on existing successful programs and activities.

- Design a district system for the identification of students at risk of dropping out. Until a local identification system is developed within a local district, a good start is to "borrow" or adapt another district's checklist.

- Involve teachers at every level to create a sense of ownership which leads to success. Invite all teachers to volunteer to participate in at-risk program activities. Involve school staff in the planning and implementation of dropout prevention efforts.

- Staff development should be provided for all certified personnel in an attempt to develop an understanding of students at risk, including the characteristics and identification of potential dropouts, and strategies to meet the needs of these students.

- Develop a "guidance team" or "case management" approach to the identification of potential student dropouts, and formation of recommendations for them. The team could be constructed similarly to special education staffing teams.

- Involve a total spectrum of resources including: outside and inside social services; nurses; social workers; psychologists; teachers from special education, Chapter 1, vocational education, and alternative education; health and social service agencies; police departments; drug and alcohol rehabilitation; businesses and community organizations.

- Develop a comprehensive and consistent district-wide attendance process that can be computerized to identify, track, and keep records on students who exhibit attendance problems. Information can then be supplied to school principals.

- Create mentorships using business and community persons with school district personnel. A multiyear commitment is important, involving interaction with the total family.

- Build business and community partnerships in activities such as Adopt-a-School, Adopt-a-Student, mentoring, and tutoring.

- Encourage students' employers to develop incentives for students to remain in school.

- Prepare news releases for school and local media.

- Involve school staff in evaluation/feedback activities.

- Develop an evaluation system for all at-risk programs, systems, and activities.

- Develop interagency councils.

- Keep dropout programs small.

- Ask for a small group of two to four teachers (volunteers) to work in a school-within-a-school situation. Ask for volunteers when staffing alternative programs.

- Develop a home/school liaison program where a teacher or social worker is assigned to help students at risk and their families communicate with the school and other agencies.

- Develop before- and after-school programs as well as Saturday classes.

- Provide staff development in building positive interpersonal relations and avoiding adversarial situations.

- Develop a plan with law enforcement officials to help monitor visitor traffic at school.

RECOMMENDATIONS FOR CURRICULUM DEVELOPMENT

- Ask school staff to assist in curriculum development and selection of resources/materials for use with dropout-prone students.

- Curriculum-related programs for students at risk should be comprised of, but not limited to: (1) academic remediation (laboratory) programs, (2) affective education, to include self-concept development and interpersonal and life skills, and (3) study skills, in addition to (4) positive school climate, (5) counseling, (6) student assistance programs, (7) peer tutoring, (8) cooperative learning teams, (9) a clearly understood discipline system, and (10) a transition system for students changing grades, schools, or classes.

- Develop preschool programs that include early teacher/parent contact, frequent teacher/parent communication, parent groups, and small classes.

- Use at-risk students as tutors in cross-age or peer tutoring programs.

- Develop a peer counseling program.

- Provide vocational education programs, encouraging an opportunity for all students to participate. Link vocational programs with strong academic courses to provide a well-rounded educational experience, and the opportunity to succeed in future employment endeavors.

- Provide broad-based career education in early grades, incorporating community experiences.

- Develop mini-courses using learning modules and computer-assisted instruction.

- Reinforce worksite experiences with classroom activities to increase value to students.

- Include involvement in local governance (school boards, public or private sector advisory boards), local crime prevention, and neighborhood clean-ups in community-based experiences.

RECOMMENDATIONS FOR TEACHERS

- Take a personal interest in one or two students both in school and outside of school through an advisement or Adopt-a-Student program.

- "Adopt a student" for the entire time the student attends school in that particular building; then, help to ease the transition to the next school by taking him/her to visit the school, meet with some teachers, and help the student identify the next person to "adopt" him or her.

- Visit students' homes prior to the beginning of school and develop a closer home/school relationships.

- Provide experiential opportunities for students.

- Allow choices and autonomous decisions by students; empower students.

- Insure the instructional value of academic activities.

- Develop an affective/social skills program and practice skills in all activities throughout the day, including the workplace.

- Adapt activities to student interest.

- Program for success.

- Ensure that students are challenged.

- Have class meetings regularly to discuss projects, changes, student-generated ideas or concerns, behavior, etc.

- Utilize community youth service agences (Job Corps, Youth Conservation Corps, Job Training Partnership Act [JTPA]).

- Involve students in creating curricular activities.

- Use media for classroom activities, such as videotaping class assignments.

- Utilize community resources for students.

- Provide incentives for student achievement.

- Integrate thinking skills and problem solving into classroom routine.

- Develop a continuous progress management system for basic skills, used along with cooperative learning.

- Provide positive classroom environment (safe and secure) — every student is worthwhile.

- Have high but attainable student expectations.

- Organize a peer calling system where by students encourage each other to attend when absent.

- Portray loving attitudes and have high expectations for students.

RECOMMENDATIONS FOR
THE SCHOOL

- Develop a positive, caring school climate for all students and staff.

- Generate an attitude of caring for students and a general atmosphere of "I am/we are interested in you as a student and individual" within the school.

- Utilize flexible class schedules to meet the needs of students at risk.

- Develop a support system for students new to school.

- Develop incentives for good attendance.

- Provide counseling groups for students.

- Form networks of community agency resources.

- Establish "rap" sessions — students with students, students with teachers, students with counselors, teachers with parents.

- Involve students in extracurricular activities and school projects.

- Involve students in community services (e.g., a class adopting a senior citizens' home to visit on a regular basis).

- Develop a proactive comprehensive student management plan with input from students, faculty, administration, and parents.

- Develop a defined discipline system, involving students in its creation.

- Provide student assistance programs for issues such as drug abuse, suicide, anorexia, bulimia, loss.

RECOMMENDATIONS FOR PARENT INVOLVEMENT

- Have parents participate on advisory committees, task forces, or assessment/evaluation teams.

- Invite and encourage parents to help at school.

- Request school staff to call parents when a potential dropout has done something "good," not only when there is a problem.

- Make ongoing or current parenting skills classes accessible and inviting to parents of dropout-prone students.

- Focus on family involvement activities that include aunts, uncles, cousins, or whoever may be available for the student.

- Find out from parents where they would like to meet about student progress (an alternative location from the school).

- Design class-written parent newsletters with follow-up activities that parents can do at home with students.

RECOMMENDATIONS FOR TRANSITIONS FROM SCHOOL TO WORK

- Invite students in dropout prevention programs and students who have left school to talk about their jobs, what they do, the type of people they work with, and working conditions.

- Invite workers to talk to students about their jobs, the need for a high school disploma, and usefulness of an education.

- Invite dropouts to talk with classes about their experiences working without a diploma.

- Ask students to identify a community service, job shadowing experience, or work partnership project for credit.

Appendix A

Dropout Identification Checklists

CHECKLIST FOR IDENTIFYING THE POTENTIAL DROPOUT

Note: This list is taken from the report of the Juvenile Delinquency Project, William C. Kvaraceus, director, *N.A.A. of the U.S., Vol. 2, Principals and Practices*, pp. 101, 102, 959, where it is "reproduced by permission of the University of the State of New York."

FACTOR	VULNERABLE TO DROPPING OUT	FAVORABLE TO COMPLETING SCHOOL
1. Age	[ ] Old for grade group (over 2 years)	[ ] At age for grade group
2. Physical size	[ ] Small for age group [ ] Large for age group	[ ] No size demarcation
3. Health	[ ] Frequently ill [ ] Fatigues easily	[ ] Consistently in good health
4. Participation in out-of-school activities	[ ] None	[ ] Planned and reasonable
5. Participation in school	[ ] None	[ ] Planned and reasonable
6. Grade retardation	[ ] One year or more retarded	[ ] At grade or above
7. Father's occupation	[ ] Unskilled [ ] Semiskilled	[ ] Professional [ ] Semiprofessional [ ] Managerial
8. Education level achieved by:		
Father	[ ] Grade 7 or below	[ ] Grade 10 or above
Mother	[ ] Grade 7 or below	[ ] Grade 10 or above
9. Number of children in family	[ ] Five or more	[ ] Three or less
10. School-to-school transfers	[ ] Pattern of "jumping" from school to school	[ ] Few or no transfers
11. Attendance	[ ] Chronic absenteeism (20 days or more per year)	[ ] Seldom absent (10 days or less per year)
12. Learning rate	[ ] IQ below 90	[ ] IQ above 100
13. Ability to read	[ ] Two or more years below grade level	[ ] At or above grade level
14. School marks	[ ] Predominantly below "C"	[ ] Predominantly "B" or above
15. Reaction to school controls	[ ] Resents controls	[ ] Willingly accepts controls
16. Acceptance by pupils	[ ] Not liked	[ ] Well liked
17. Parental attitude toward graduation	[ ] Negative [ ] Vacillating	[ ] Positive [ ] United
18. Pupil interest in school work	[ ] Little or none	[ ] High
19. General adjustment	[ ] Fair or poor	[ ] Good

Source: California State Department of Education, *California Curriculum News Report*, October 1986.

WHAT IS YOUR SCHOOL CLIMATE?

Is your school's atmosphere conducive to making pupils feel good about coming to their school? Below is a checklist that may assist you in determining if your school contributes to a positive school climate.

	Yes	No	Needs Attn.
• Does our school have strategies for early intervention with uninvolved, isolated, socially-lost pupils?	[ ]	[ ]	[ ]
• Does our school have easy accessibility to all teachers or administrators?	[ ]	[ ]	[ ]
• Are our pupils proud of their school?	[ ]	[ ]	[ ]
• Does our school reflect a feeling of caring and trust?	[ ]	[ ]	[ ]
• Do our pupils feel that what they are learning is important to their future and current personal lives?	[ ]	[ ]	[ ]
• Are our pupils accountable for our codes of behavior?	[ ]	[ ]	[ ]
• Does our school have clearly stated goals?	[ ]	[ ]	[ ]
• Does our school have a complete and understandable discipline policy?	[ ]	[ ]	[ ]
• Does our school have a complete and understandable attendance policy?	[ ]	[ ]	[ ]
• Is the feeling of the community supportive of our school's efforts?	[ ]	[ ]	[ ]
• Is our discipline administered in a firm, fair, and consistent manner?	[ ]	[ ]	[ ]
• Does a plan exist in our school to reduce vandalism?	[ ]	[ ]	[ ]
• Is there a philosophy in our school that discipline is everyone's responsibility, not just an administration/counseling one?	[ ]	[ ]	[ ]
• Do teachers in our school contact parents on a regular basis?	[ ]	[ ]	[ ]
• Are there reasonable alternatives to suspension in our school?	[ ]	[ ]	[ ]
• Are pupils apprehensive about their personal safety in halls, restrooms, and lunch area?	[ ]	[ ]	[ ]

Source: *The Prevention of Truancy: Programs and Strategies That Address the Problems of Truancy and Dropouts*, Los Angeles County Office of Education, 1986 (out of print).

HOW MUCH DO YOU KNOW
ABOUT YOUR PUPILS?

The following list contains many characteristics of pupils who have dropped out of school. Please check (X) those characteristics that describe high risk pupils and dropouts in *your* school district. Check all that apply.

[ ] poor grades overall

[ ] low math scores

[ ] failed in other schools

[ ] low perceptual performance in one or more areas

[ ] verbal deficiency

[ ] gifted and/or talented abilities, but bored with school

[ ] been retained a grade

[ ] expressed feelings of not belonging in school

[ ] poor social adjustment

[ ] fails to see relevance of education to the life experience

[ ] frequent health problems

[ ] acts socially or emotionally disturbed

[ ] general unacceptance by school staff

[ ] father/parent absent from home

[ ] generally not accepted by his/her peers ("a loner")

[ ] low income family/serious economic problems

[ ] low or inappropriate self-concept

[ ] frequent truancy

[ ] low reading scores

[ ] no future orientation

[ ] immature, suggestible, easily distracted behaviors

[ ] inability to identify with others

[ ] inability to tolerate structured activities

[ ] lack of identity with school

[ ] inability to relate to authority figures

[ ] disruptive behaviors

[ ] inability to function properly within traditional classroom

[ ] been emotionally neglected

[ ] rebellious attitudes toward authority

[ ] friends who are mostly older and out of school

[ ] non-English speaking home

[ ] siblings or parents who have been dropouts

[ ] has moved more than other students

[ ] frequent contacts with police

Source: *The Prevention of Truancy: Programs and Strategies That Address the Problems of Truancy and Dropouts*, Los Angeles County Office of Education, 1986 (out of print).

EARLY IDENTIFICATION OF
A POTENTIAL DROPOUT

Check only those areas that apply to the named individual.

NAME_____ GRADE_____ DATE_____

NON-SCHOOL-RELATED FACTORS

[ ] Poor social adjustment, perhaps socially and emotionally disturbed

[ ] Low perceptual performance

[ ] Low self-concept/low level of self-esteem

[ ] Immature, suggestible, easily distracted, lack of future orientation

[ ] Frequent health problems

[ ] Alcohol or drug problems

[ ] Unable to identify with peers, teachers

[ ] Friends are outside of school, usually older

SCHOOL-RELATED FACTORS

[ ] Early absenteeism/truancy

[ ] Frequent tardiness

[ ] Achievement below grade level; failing classes/low test scores

[ ] Verbal deficiency

[ ] Failure in one or more schools

[ ] Disruptive behavior and/or rebellious attitudes

[ ] Classified as slow learners (IQs of 75-90)

[ ] Lack of basic skills

[ ] Has repeated at least one grade

[ ] Older than classmates

[ ] Limited extracurricular participation

[ ] Lack of identification with school; feeling of not belonging

[ ] Failure to see relevance of education — uninterested

[ ] Dissatisfaction with teachers

[ ] Feelings of rejection by school — feelings of alienation

[ ] Unable to tolerate structured activities

[ ] Friends are outside of school

FAMILY-RELATED FACTORS

[ ] Communication between home and school is usually poor

[ ] Absence of father/mother from home

[ ] Non-English speaking home

[ ] Frequent residential changes

[ ] Family violence (physical or sexual abuse)

[ ] Siblings or parents have been dropouts

[ ] Family disturbances

[ ] Tend to come from low-income families

Source: *The Prevention of Truancy: Programs and Strategies That Address the Problems of Truancy and Dropouts*, Los Angeles County Office of Education, 1986 (out of print).

DROPOUT IDENTIFICATION SURVEY

| _____ | Lower Elementary [ ] | | | | Upper Elementary [ ] |
| Respondent's District | Junior High/Middle School [ ] | | | | High School [ ] |

Factor	School	Home	Community	Grade Level	Source of Identification
Academic Difficulty (especially reading)					
Grade Failure					
Need Money					
Get Married					
English Language Difficulty					
School Discipline Problem					
Poor Attendance					
Peer Pressure					
Alienation/Isolation					
Boredom/Lack of Interest					
Pregnancy					
Dislike School					
School Seen as Unimportant					
Home Stress					
Substance Abuse					
Health Problems					
Feel Harassed by School					
Single Parent Family					
Poor Self-Concept					
Emotional Problems					
No Participation in Extra-curricular Activities					
Family History of Dropouts					
Frequent Moves					

Source: "Dropout Prevention Survey," Oakland County Schools, Pontiac, Michigan, May 1985.

POTENTIAL SCHOOL
DROPOUT FORM

Name of Student _____ Grade Level _____ Date _____

Referring Teacher _____ School _____

Identified exceptionality (if appropriate) _____

Listed below are characteristics of potential school dropouts. Please check the appropriate column box for each characteristic. In addition, check the appropriate column for the characteristics you think are significantly impacting on the student's potential to be a school dropout. At the end of each section is a space for you to write pertinent comments.

I. FACTUAL CHARACTERISTICS

School:

Number of Days   Absent / Tardy

1. Irregular attendance and/or frequent tardiness.

First 9 weeks   _____   _____
Second 9 weeks   _____   _____
Third 9 weeks   _____   _____
Fourth 9 weeks   _____   _____

2. Failure — School Years

Number school years retained _____
Retained in current grade   [ ]   Yes
                            [ ]   No

3. Student lacks basic skills necessary for success.

A. Check appropriate areas where basic skills are deficient:

[ ] Reading   [ ] Comm. Skills

[ ] Writing   [ ] Mathematics

[ ] Spelling   [ ] Other _____

B. California Achievement Test Scores

Composite percentile _____ %

4. Failure — School Subjects

Number of school subjects students is currently failing _____

Teacher Comments (Items 1-4): _____

_____

_____

(Form continues on page 42.)

Family:

5. Educational level of parents below high school level.

    A. Did father graduate from high school?
[ ] Yes [ ] No [ ] Information Unknown

    B. Did mother graduate from high school?
[ ] Yes [ ] No [ ] Information Unknown

6. Family patterns of dropping out of school.

    A. Number of brothers/sisters in family

    _____ .

    B. Number of brothers/sisters dropping out of school:

    ____Brothers ____Sisters ____Information Unknown

7. Miscellaneous family characteristics.

    A. Are parents divorced?
[ ] Yes [ ] No [ ] Information Unknown

    B. Does child live in a one-parent household?
[ ] Yes [ ] No [ ] Information Unknown

    C. Does child live with a stepfather or stepmother?
[ ] Yes [ ] No [ ] Information Unknown

    D. Does child live in family situation other than with parents (grandparents, foster care, etc.)?
[ ] Yes [ ] No [ ] Information Unknown

    E. Is there a history of frequent family moves/changes in school?
[ ] Yes [ ] No [ ] Information Unknown

    F. Is the child's family currently receiving economic assistance in government sources (food stamps, AFDC, etc.)?
[ ] Yes [ ] No [ ] Information Unknown

Teacher Comments (Items 5-7) _____

_____

_____

II. OBSERVABLE CHARACTERISTICS

	Occasionally Observed	Frequently Observed	Unobserved and/or Not Applicable	Significant Problem

School

1. Performance consistently below potential.

2. Pattern of disruptive/ aggressive behavior.

3. Poor study/work habits (attention span, test-taking ability).

4. Little or no participation in extracurricular or special interest activities.

5. Poor self-concept (with-drawn, lack of friends, feeling of not belonging, etc.).

Teacher Comments: _____

_____

_____

	Occasionally Observed	Frequently Observed	Unobserved and/or Not Applicable	Significant Problem

Family

6. Parents not educationally supportive of their child.

7. Parents not educationally supportive of their child's teacher/administrators.

8. Unhappy family situation (neglect, abuse, emotional upheaval, lack of discipline, minimal family solidarity).

9. Few family friends.

(Form continues on page 44.)

Teacher Comments: _____

_____

_____

	Occasionally Observed	Frequently Observed	Unobserved and/or Not Applicable	Significant Problem

Personal/Peers

10. Friends not school oriented (friends not in school, former dropouts). _____

11. Friends not approved by parents. _____

12. Alcohol/drug abuse. _____

13. Physical health problems (chronic illness, obesity, physical deformity, pregnancy, etc.). _____

Other Comments: _____

_____

_____

Any additional information not covered in this form_____

_____

_____

_____

_____

_____

_____

Source: Granville County (North Carolina) School System, 1985.

Appendix B

Program
Descriptions

CURRICULUM-RELATED PROGRAMS, INCLUDING EARLY CHILDHOOD

TITLE OF PROGRAM/Curriculum
Pre-Kindergarten Summer School Program (Wisconsin)

Level (Pre-Kindergarten)

Description
All kindergarten students coming in fall attend for two weeks. Used primarily for informational purposes and for adjustment to school setting. Some attend for six weeks if screening process identified them as having potential academic/social difficulties.

Contact Person
Kenneth Baroun
Mishicot School District
Mishicot, WI 54338
414-755-2391

● —————— ● —————— ●

TITLE OF PROGRAM/Curriculum
Green Bay Head Start Program (Wisconsin)

Level (Pre-Kindergarten)

Description
The primary goal of the Green Bay Head Start Program is to provide a comprehensive developmental program for three- and four-year-old preschool children from low-income families. The program is based on the philosophy that every child can benefit from an interdisciplinary approach to foster development, provided through the broad range of services for children and their parents. Services provided are in the areas of: education, health, mental health, nutrition, social services, and parent involvement.

The Green Bay Head Start Program has two components:

1. *Center-Based Program*
   In this component, the children attend the center in a school setting two and three-fourths hours per day, three days per week. The remainder of time is basically utilized to involve parents in activities with their children. Each participating family receives a minimum of three home visits per year.

2. *Home-Based Program*
   In this component, the children attend the center in a school setting two and three-fourths hours per day, one day per week. However, each participating family in this component receives one home visit per week.

Contact Person
> Jerry Whitehouse
> Green Bay School District
> 200 South Broadway
> P.O. Box 1387
> Green Bay, WI 54305
> 414-497-3956

• —————— • —————— •

TITLE OF PROGRAM/Curriculum
> Handicapped Child Find and Pre-School Program (Colorado)

Level (Preschool)

Description
> This program serves handicapped students who are four years of age (as mandated under PL 94-142). It provides one year of remedial and compensatory services prior to the child's eligibility for school-aged service. The program focuses on developmental skills. Children to be served have been identified through the District's Child-Find process.
> The Early Childhood program provides one morning class and one afternoon class of 12 students each. It is staffed by one teacher, one aide, and related services in physical therapy, speech therapy, and vision.

Contact Person
> Shirley Wells, Consultant
> Department of Special Education
> Aurora Public Schools
> 11023 East 5th Avenue
> Aurora, CO 80010
> 303-340-0510

• —————— • —————— •

TITLE OF PROGRAM/Curriculum
> Plattsburgh Follow Through Program (New York)

Level (Elementary)

Description
> Approved by JDRP (Joint Dissemination and Review Panel) for grades kindergarten through third, the goals of the Plattsburgh Follow Through program are to prevent economically disadvantaged children from failing in reading and math and to promote development of their language skills. Initial and ongoing assessment, weekly meetings of the entire staff, periodic reviews of each child's reading and math programs, and staff development in Bank Street College of Education theories and practices are the means used to attain the program's goals.
> Rather than being directed by their teacher, the children help shape their own activities. They work independently, in small groups, or singly with the teacher or aide on such projects as sand and block construction, art activities, cooking, dictation, journal writing, measurement, and science experiments. The classroom setting is tightly organized, giving

children the opportunity to express themselves in words and actions and to work with each other.

Home visits, trips for parents and children, and participation by parents in the classroom are fundamental to the program. Parents are also actively involved in decisionmaking in all aspects of the program. In addition, parents are offered a variety of practical and academic courses and workshops with community agencies.

Contact Person
Thelma Dodson, Director
Plattsburgh Follow Through Program
Monty Street School
Monty Street
Plattsburgh, NY 12901
518-563-1140

• ———— • ———— •

TITLE OF PROGRAM/Curriculum
Discovery Through Reading (Michigan)

Level (Elementary)

Description
Discovery Through Reading is a JDRP-validated program that stresses rapid skill development for second- and third-grade students who are having difficulty in their regular classrooms. Goals include the improvement of students' ability to recognize words and improvement of their reading comprehension. In the Discovery project, teachers work with two students at a time in 45-minute sessions scheduled twice weekly at a location outside the regular classroom. Each full-time Discovery teacher's maximum case load is 30 students. A key organizational feature of instruction is the "task sheet," an agenda that lists six specific activities to be completed by a student during each session. The task sheet helps teachers decide what tasks are within the capabilities of students. An important aspect of the project is the way in which teachers interact with students, providing students with a nonthreatening environment. A student competes only with himself/herself, and performance and achievement are reinforced with concrete rewards. All activities are charted and graphed immediately, showing teacher and student that progress is being made and that goals are being achieved.

Evaluation gains over the years are consistently higher than the average. Evaluation results for the 1988-89 school year (spring-to-spring test cycle) are as follows: District aggregate gain in comprehension was 22 NCEs for second, third, and fourth grades. Second grade - 18.1 NCEs, third grade - 20.3 NCEs, fourth grade - 27.5 NCEs.

Contact Person
Dorothy Neff, Project Director
Clarkston Community Schools
6590 Middle Lake Road
Clarkston, MI 48016
313-625-3330

• ———— • ———— •

TITLE OF PROGRAM/Curriculum
Early Success in School (California)

Level (Elementary)
Kindergarten through third grade

Description
 The program emphasized the prevention of early school failure rather than just its remediation. The focus is on expanding kindergarten through third grade curriculum to provide classroom activities that foster children's thinking skills and allow the children to develop more positive attitudes toward themselves and their school work. Early Success in School was featured at the Sharing Educational Success Traveling Seminars in 1982.

Contact Person
Hugh Cox, Ph.D., Director
or Carol Swain, Coordinator
P.O. Box 13
Corte Modera, CA 94925
415-794-3821

TITLE OF PROGRAM/Curriculum
Transitional Class Program (Miami, Dade County School District, Florida)

Level (Elementary)

Description
 Grades 1-6 students who have failed to pass a grade are diagnosed and a prescribed program is designed for them.
 The instruction in the transitional class is concentrated in the basic skills areas and students are provided with remedial instruction in the areas of previous academic failure. When appropriate, students are mainstreamed into regular classes at the grade level to which the student would have been assigned if promoted.
 The transitional class concept focuses on alternative strategies to prevent failure. It provides many students the opportunity to gain the skills they lack for promotion in a much shorter time and in a more efficient manner.

Contact Person
Mary Vareen, Coordinator of Programs
Miami, Dade County School District
1410 N.E. 2nd Avenue
Miami, FL 33132
305-376-1755

TITLE OF PROGRAM/Curriculum
Mentorship Program (Oregon)

Level (Elementary)

Description

      Mentorship program with students to be connected with adults in businesses and public schools. "Mentorship" began in Santa Clara elementary as a pilot, and is now in four elementaries. The program identifies students having difficulties in school and ties them with an adult (surrogate parent). The program also encourages mentors among parents, teachers, parents of other children, and employees of school.

      Mentorship Model: Mentorship (or advocacy) programs are one proven way of establishing a bonding relationship between students and their homan institutions—schools. Mentors help create a bond that some students have not otherwise found.

      Our goals as mentors are to:

1. Facilitate a sense of belonging—the sense that someone cares.

2. Encourage a commitment to the educational process.

3. Strengthen a belief in self.

4. Promote an involvement in the social life of the school and community.

Contact Person

Bob Stalick
Eugene Public Schools
200 North Monroe
Eugene, OR 97402
503-687-3123

● ———— ● ———— ●

TITLE OF PROGRAM/Curriculum

Kindergarten Reinforcement (Ohio)

Level (Elementary)

Description

      The Kindergarten Reinforcement Project is designed to:

- Meet the needs of children early, thus improving their readiness for learning

- Increase the involvement of parents in the education of their children

- Improve the professional skills of staff to meet the needs of children

- Prepare children for success in school

- Expand on gains made in Child Development.

      There are approximately 6,000 children per year, 5 years of age, who need educationally enriching experiences. The Centers are located in 82 selected elementary schools in poverty areas of Cleveland.

      The staff consists of Project coordinator, experienced teachers, 37 educational aides (selected schools), teacher consultants, reading specialist, social worker/visiting teachers, clerks, and parent and community volunteers.

Regular kindergarten children attend class one-half day, five days each week. Full-day kindergarten (pilot) children attend class five hours, five days each week.

Parent involvement and teacher staff inservice training and coordination with other programs are all ongoing activities in the Project.

An augmented curriculum is offered for the children and enriched by new instructional games, toys, and devices, more individualized instruction, speech improvement program in selected schools, health and dental education, and emphasis on pre-reading and mathematics activities. Pilot projects in selected schools provide computer instruction and bilingual services.

For parents, classroom observations, volunteering, meetings, and workshops are available. There are booklets and printed materials for home use with children. Opportunities to assist in classrooms, on committees, and on trips enhance parents' involvement in the project.

For teachers, there are differentiated inservice workshops, group meetings, demonstrations, individual in-class counseling, consultants, and a staff specialist on call.

Supportive services for Kindergarten Reinforcement include a visiting teacher (social worker); psychological aid; medical, speech, and dental check-ups; referrals; and health education.

Contact Person
Emma Benning, Assistant Superintendent
Cleveland Public Schools
4380 East 6th Street
Cleveland, OH 44114
216-574-8666

●───────●───────●

TITLE OF PROGRAM/Curriculum
Resident Study Project (Ohio)

Level   (Elementary)

Description
The Resident Study Project is designed to provide students an opportunity to participate in resident educational programming, leadership orientation, and field studies. It also provides educational and environmental experiences that cannot or would not be met within the normal school day or environment. Resident Study also provides urban students an extended classroom experience in a natural environment in order to increase their understanding of the interrelationship between nature and humankind.

The pupil population consists of sixth-grade homeroom units and leadership and field study students. The students are from qualified Chapter 1 schools. The staff of the Project is made up of a Project coordinator, a resource staff of experts and specialists, educational aides, a clerk, and two or three homeroom teachers per session.

Project activities are centered in an agency camp/field study sites within a 50-mile radius of Greater Cleveland, and the Cuyahoga Valley National Recreation Area.

Resident Study's curriculum consists of a continuity of instruction in the major elementary subject areas, utilizing the environment with a focus on Adventure Education through science, mathematics, and language arts experiences. The Project runs from September through mid-December and from February through May. Students leave their home school on Tuesday, live at camp 24 hours daily, return to their home school on Thursday or as scheduled.

Contact Person
Emma Benning, Assistant Superintendent
Cleveland Public Schools
4380 East 6th Street
Cleveland, OH 44114
216-574-8666

● ———— ● ———— ●

TITLE OF PROGRAM/Curriculum
Transitional K-1 (Wisconsin)

Level (Elementary)

Description
The transitional program was founded on the premise that a child should not repeat kindergarten. The program will give selected students an additional year of readiness after kindergarten to prepare them for successful learning of basic skills while progressing through the grades. It is necessary to limit class size so as to accommodate the program.

Students are selected on the basis of teacher-made tests and teacher observation. A total evaluation of social, physical, and academic growth provides a basis for final decision.

Intervention Techniques:

1. A full daily plan of instruction.

2. Curriculum unique to each child and based upon the individual student's total social, physical, psychological, and academic growth and development.

3. Special emphasis on basic psychomotor skill development.

4. Emphasize basic academic readiness skills.

5. Emphasize oral language and increase speaking vocabulary.

6. Emphasize movement skills to develop fine and large motor skills.

7. Emphasize time on task comprehension necessary to academic instruction.

8. Special development in creative dramatics and role playing.

9. Strongly emphasize development of self-confidence, self-worth, and acceptance of realities of life situations.

10. Continuing evaluation and assessment program for each child.

11. Strong teacher-parent involvement program.

Contact Person
Kenneth Baroun
Mishicot School District
Mishicot, WI 54338
414-755-2391

●————————●————————●

TITLE OF PROGRAM/Curriculum
Developmental Guidance K-6 (Wisconsin)

Level (Elementary)

Description
The O. H. Schultz Elementary School Developmental Guidance Program is considered an important part of the "Child at Risk" Program.

The program operates on the concept that students will meet regularly in large- and small-group sessions with the elementary school guidance counselor. The counselor will use a planned program to help students deal with personal feelings, understand their role and responsibility as a student or member of a group, and how to make responsible decisions. While working with students, the counselor can identify students that could benefit from individual guidance activity or sessions.

Goals of the program are:

1. Maintain student interest in school.

2. Motivate students and encourage students to try to be successful in school and out of school.

3. Assist students in coping with problems both in and out of school.

4. Help students see the value of attending school.

5. Develop skills in the decisionmaking process.

6. Develop the self-image of each student.

7. Develop an awareness and understanding of careers and opportunities that are available.

8. Develop the concept and importance of lifelong learning.

Contact Person
Kenneth Baroun
Mishicot School District
Mishicot, WI 54338
414-755-2391

●————————●————————●

TITLE OF PROGRAM/Curriculum
Developmental Kindergarten (Colorado)

Level (Elementary)

Description
The Developmental Kindergarten was created out of a need to give students at risk of school failure one year of intensive developmental

curriculum prior to entering the first grade. The program is comprised of special needs students, those identified as handicapped with one or more labels, regular education students, and some open enrolled students from other schools who are not identified as handicapped, but who are identified as at high risk for failure in regular kindergarten classes.

Two full-time teachers, one special education and one general education teacher, and a full-time paraprofessional work with a maximum of 25 to 28 students per session in this collaborative model. Of the 25 students, 8 maximum are identified as handicapped. As the school is on a year-round schedule, students have only short periods of time out of school, which may enable them not to lose information gained.

The program components include highly manipulative hands-on materials, functional curriculum involving "community experiences," i.e., field trips, and a whole-language approach. Parents, students, teachers, and school administration are pleased with the results at present. Students who were identified as high-risk have been very successful with the program.

Contact Person
Shirley Wells, Consultant
Department of Special Education
Aurora Public Schools
11023 East 5th Avenue
Aurora, CO 80010
303-340-0510

● —————— ● —————— ●

TITLE OF PROGRAM/Curriculum
Assessment and Support (PAS) (Colorado)

Level (Elementary)

Description
On June 23, 1979, the Board of Education unanimously approved a proposal to add certified teachers to certain elementary schools to support the K-1 Primary Curriculum. This assistance to the regular classroom teacher resulted in more effective instruction to be given to identified students to prevent gaps in their learning.

Program features include:

1. Identification of kindergarten and first-grade children who need intensive instruction through small-group and/or individual work.

2. Teamwork and a sense of purpose directed to the child's learning among kindergarten, first-grade, and PAS teachers.

3. Diagnostic/prescriptive instruction.

4. Long- and short-range objectives for supplemental instruction.

5. Flexible groupings for instruction.

6. Periodic Primary Team meetings including the principal, kindergarten, first-grade, and PAS teacher.

7. A focus on the curricular areas of mathematics and reading.

8. A management system to monitor student progress regularly.

9. Ongoing staff development as need dictates.

Contact Person
Jane Needham, Ed.D., Elementary
    Curriculum Coordinator
Aurora Public Schools
1085 Peoria
Aurora, CO 80011
303-344-8060

●　————　●　————　●

TITLE OF PROGRAM/Curriculum
Child Study Team (CARES) (Colorado)

Level　(Elementary, Middle School)

Description
    These teams, known as Child Study Teams or Teacher Assistance Teams, are comprised largely of general education teachers with one or two special education personnel. The goal is to provide educational/emotional/behavioral support to students as a step before making a referral to special education.

    The team generates possible intervention strategies to use in the regular classroom, considering teachers' resources and style. The best of these intervention strategies are presented to the teacher by a team member. The team members assist and support the teacher during implementation of the intervention(s). By providing such assistance, they provide indirect services to students.

    Team objectives:

1. Brainstorm instructional ideas for teachers, in order to reduce special education referrals.

2. Find solutions to problems by examining the student's environment, and not treating the child's difficulty strictly as an internal problem.

3. Provide support and assistance to teachers of students who are experiencing academic and/or behavioral problems.

4. Broaden the options for students who are not performing desirably in the classroom.

Contact Person
Suzanne Johnson
Lyn Knoll/Paris Elementary School
12445 East 2nd Avenue
Aurora, CO 80011
303-364-8455/344-1702

●　————　●　————　●

TITLE OF PROGRAM/Curriculum
Suspend a Student; Invite a Parent (Delaware)

Level (Elementary, Middle, High School)

Description
Lake Forest School District uses a new approach in handling discipline problems. Students who would normally experience suspension may now avoid that exit from the classroom provided they agree to bring their parents to school for a day. The district believes students should not be out of class, but should also exhibit proper behavior while in class. The program is limited to nonviolent disruptions. Suspensions for weapons, drug or alcohol violation, and other serious offenses must still be served.

The program serves three purposes. First, with the parent in the room, behavior will improve; communications between the school and the home will be enhanced; and students will not miss as much class time.

Parent reaction to the program has been positive. Some students felt it might be embarrassing to have their parents attend school with them. Students whose parents participated, however, felt good about the program.

Contact Person
James H. VanSciver, Ed.D., Superintendent
Lake Forest School District
Harrington, DE 19952
302-398-3244

● ———— ● ———— ●

TITLE OF PROGRAM/Curriculum
Alternate Skills (Wisconsin)

Level (Middle School)
Children who have failed required classes in social studies and English

Description
The district operates an alternate skills class that serves to aid students who have failed required classes in social studies or English.

The course is developed around the improvement of basic skills with a strong emphasis toward the development of a positive self-image and study skills improvement.

The class usually enrolls from three to eight students who have failed at least one semester.

Successful completion of a semester allows the student to earn one half credit, while at the same time eliminating a prior failure. The "clincher" is the fact that while the student is enrolled in the class, the student must receive passing grades in all of his/her other courses.

Standards for success in the class are regular attendance and completion of assignments when due.

The class meets four times weekly and, in addition, students spend three to five periods in a closely supervised study group. Emphasis is placed on group dynamics, class visitors, and assessment of healthy attendance.

Contact Person
Mike Willems, Guidance Counselor
Clear Lake School District
Clear Lake, WI 54005
715-263-2113

• ——— • ——— •

TITLE OF PROGRAM/Curriculum
Learning Lab (Oregon)

Level   (Middle Level)

Description
This self-contained program provides hands-on activities that are designed to help the middle-school-age child develop academic and interpersonal skills. The field-oriented design stresses an interdisciplinary approach to the areas of life, earth, and social sciences as well as the academic needs of the students.

Each unit of study focuses on developing a sense of responsibility and belonging and is designed to create an atmosphere of excitement, challenge, and success.

The basic skills of reading, writing, and English are incorporated into courses such as marine biology, horticulture, and animal studies. Math courses are taken within the regular school setting.

The program works on establishing positive learning attitudes before absenteeism, negative attitudes, and poor academic performance become permanent behavior patterns. The staff works with the students to help them choose positive learning experiences at this stage of their lives. Students participate in group counseling.

Contact Person
Alcena Boozer, Alternative Education
    Supervisor
Portland Public Schools
P.O. Box 3107
Portland, OR 97208
503-280-5783

• ——— • ——— •

TITLE OF PROGRAM/Curriculum
Pelham Magnet Middle School (Michigan)

Level   (Middle School, High School)

Description
The Pelham Magnet Middle School has the "human touch" in its responsibility to help students develop:

• Basic math skills

• Basic language skills

• A source for reinforcement of these skills

• Skills in decision-making and goal-setting

- Successful skills in human relationships
- Self-awareness insights
  - An understanding of physical and mental development processes
  - An acceptance of one's own physical and mental development.

A positive self-image is developed through an understanding of:

- Personal areas of interest
- Personal strengths and weaknesses
- Personal career desires
- Personal aptitudes and abilities
- Personal values and feelings.

English, math, and social studies are courses required of all students each semester.

Two years of science are required and usually completed in grades six and seven. For the students with special talent and interest in science, an advanced science class is offered to eighth grade students. Students in advanced science prepare entries for the Metropolitan Detroit Science Fair, participate in a science camp held at Camp Metamora during the spring, and are members of the Detroit Area Pre-College Engineering Program (DAP-CEP).

Contact Person
Aretha Marshall
5051 Woodward Avenue
Detroit, Michigan 48202
313-494-1087

● ———— ● ———— ●

TITLE OF PROGRAM/Curriculum
Student Advocate Program (Delaware)

Level   (Junior High)

Description
The Student Advocate Program was designed for three purposes: at-risk student identification, development of intervention programs to meet needs of identified students, and measurement of the effectiveness of the intervention. Students are identified if they have three or more failing grades in academic subjects, five or more days of unexcused absence from the beginning of the school year, and three or more discipline referrals to the school office from the beginning of the school year. The intervention procedure provides for those identified students to select one adult in the school with whom they would like to meet. That adult could be a teacher, custodian, secretary, food service employee, or administrator.

The student and advocate meet once per week for nine consecutive weeks at the discretion of the advocate. Discussion during these meetings could center on grades, attendance, behavior, self-image, or any other topic of interest to the student. The meetings are humanistic and non-threatening. Advocates meet with building-level and district administration to discuss how to anticipate questions and situations which might arise with the students.

A $1,500 grant from Delaware's Department of Public Instruction was used to underwrite the cost of meals and a culminating activity for all advocates and students. Some advocates take their students to dinner. All participate in a year-end culminating activity field trip to Great Adventure in New Jersey.

Contact Person
James H. VanSciver, Ed.D., Superintendent
Lake Forest School District
Harrington, DE 19952
302-398-3244

● —————— ● —————— ●

TITLE OF PROGRAM/Curriculum
Recognition of Student Achievement and Positive Behavior through Financial Incentives (Michigan)

Level (Middle School)
Grades six, seven, eight, and nine

Description
Recognition of student achievement and positive behavior is vital if students are to continue to desire to achieve and interact responsibly with others. Clarkston Junior High School has taken steps to recognize and award students who do behave appropriately and achieve academically. These steps are intended to encourage students to continue their growth in these areas.

STUDENT INCENTIVE PROGRAM: designed to recognize students who display excellence in the areas of academics and behavior. Students are recognized each marking period in the areas of citizenship, improvement, honor roll, and attendance. Funded by student council, five students are chosen in each category. "Winners" received gift certificates (for food) or cash.

LUNCH WITH THE PRINCIPALS: designed to recognize those students who might not receive school recognition through regular channels. Teachers may nominate students at any point throughout the school year. Names are drawn and students are then sent invitations to lunch. Students are typically nominated for good behavior. A display case features their names and pictures.

STUDENT OF THE MONTH: designed to recognize outstanding academic achievement. Students are nominated monthly and are awarded school T-shirts and certificates. Biographical information is included on a card next to their picture in a special display case.

CERTIFICATES:

- Attendance—eight hours or less absence from school year results in attendance award at honors assembly

- Honor Roll—Clarkston Junior High maintains three honor rolls (all A, B, or better per each marking period—four per year).

A variety of certificates is given, including Presidential Academic Fitness, excellence in academic areas, school spirit, and Principal's Award.

Contact Person
Duane Lewis, Principal
Clarkston Junior High School
63400 Church Street
Clarkston, MI 48016
313-625-5361

•───────•───────•

TITLE OF PROGRAM/Curriculum
Internal Suspension Room (Ohio)

Level   (Middle School, High School)

Description
The Internal Suspension Room (ISR) Project is designed to:

- Continue the regular academic work assignments while students are in the ISR

- Provide students with counseling to identify the nature of problems and the impact on their current situation

- Identify potentially serious behavioral tendencies which may require referral to guidance resources

- Support students in formulating solutions to their difficulties

- Provide communication to teachers about students' needs and the role of teachers in supporting students' adjustment to school.

The number of pupils involved in ISR ranges from 1 to 15, depending upon assignment by principal. There are classes in 36 junior and senior high schools, 1 classroom per school. The ISR staff consists of a Project coordinator and a clerk, and each class has one to three teachers, depending on the organization.

Each student assigned to the Internal Suspension Room is expected to complete all class assignments and homework assignments during the period assigned to the room.

All rooms will be equipped with subject textbooks and other materials to support the ongoing educational process of the school.

Supportive services for the Project include:

- Administrative supervision from principal

- Total school support to provide ongoing educational experiences

- Support from school and community resources upon referral

- Continuing inservice training for ISR teachers.

Contact Person
Emma Benning, Assistant Superintendent
Cleveland Public Schools
4380 East 6th Street
Cleveland, OH 44114
216-574-8666

●————————●————————●

TITLE OF PROGRAM/Curriculum
Franklin High School Reading Laboratory and Writing Laboratory
(Wisconsin)

Level (High School)
Academically disadvantaged

Description
These laboratories have been developed to provide remediation for students who have severe skills deficits in reading and writing. The program is personalized and prescriptive, and aimed at correcting problems generated when students function several grade levels below their peers in academic performance. A variety of methods is employed, including an emphasis on computer-assisted instruction.

Contact Person
Margaret Grabowski
Franklin High School
8222 South 51st Street
Franklin, WI 53132
414-421-3000

●————————●————————●

TITLE OF PROGRAM/Curriculum
Individual Learning Program (Wisconsin)

Level (High School)
Potential dropouts, economically and/or socially disadvantaged, teen parent, habitual truant

Description
This course was developed out of concern for students who are not experiencing much success in their high-school experience as evidenced by either substandard grades, insufficient credits, poor attendance habits, or a combination of these factors. This course is, therefore, designed to provide additional support for these students as a means of helping them have a more positive and productive high-school experience. The course is not open to all students. It is open only to those invited to enroll because of their previous high school experiences.
The goals of this course are:

1. To promote positive attitudes towards self and school.

2. To improve academic standing and acquire passing grades.

3. To improve attendance in all classes.

4. To help direct and acquaint students with jobs in each individual's interest.

5. To help students earn a diploma.

The courses will have three integral parts. The first will involve individual counseling to improve self-concept and motivation. The second will involve support groups from peers and teachers to raise individual academic achievement, and the third will provide training and job opportunities before and after graduation.

Course credit of one-half credit/semester will be offered to all those enrolled. Students who qualify for employment and early release will be paid hourly wages. Class instruction will consist of unique and varied opportunities, such as "Hands On" activities and trips throughout southwest Wisconsin. These activities will become an integral part of the learning process, with emphasis on real-life situations. Guest speakers and business people will be asked to share a variety of experiences and opportunities. As with any worthwhile project, there are minimum standards which must be followed. As with a regular job, no more than ten days per semester can be missed at either school or employment. Also, all grades must be raised to passing and then maintained at that level.

It is believed that the needs of these students, the school, and the community will be better served with this new program. Those students who are encountering difficulties both academically and emotionally will be helped on an individual basis. Basic life situations and experiences will be handled by experts in the field and community business people. A team of teachers and the counselor will be available throughout the day, every day, for support and guidance.

Contact Person

Sharon Curtis, Director
ILP/Counselor
Dodgeville High School
912 West Chapel Street
Dodgeville, WI 53533-1088
608-935-3307

● ———————— ● ———————— ●

TITLE OF PROGRAM/Curriculum

Secondary Learning Center Program (Missouri)

Level (High School)

Students with behavior, academic, and truancy problems

Description

Targeted at students who do not qualify for special education but who are not successful in their academic classes, including reluctant and slow learners and students at risk of dropping out or of failing courses.

The purpose of the Secondary Learning Center Program is to increase learning effectiveness through modification of the curriculum, the instructional materials, and the learning environment. Students are taught to organize and plan their learning experiences. Students in the

SLC follow the same curriculum as students in regular classes, but smaller class sizes allow for more individualized instruction and flexibility. SLC parents also meet with the student's parents and other teachers to build communication between home and school. Increased attention is given to the student's study habits and self-esteem. Students taking classes in the SLC are evaluated by the staff at the end of the grading period to determine whether they should continue in the program or return to the original classroom.

The overall goals of the Secondary Learning Center are:

- To assist students in earning graduation credits

- To reduce student absenteeism at the high school

- To accommodate varied student learning styles in order to assure success in school

- To successfully return participating students to the regular classroom.

Contact Person
Ernest Paris
Lee's Summit School District
600 Miller Street
Lee's Summit, MO 64063
816-524-2400

•————— • ————— •

TITLE OF PROGRAM/Curriculum
Re-Entry Program, Sterling Heights Senior High School (Michigan)

Level (High School)
Former dropouts, high-risk students

Description
Sterling Heights Senior High School of Warren Consolidated Schools recruits, welcomes, monitors, and supports former dropouts and other high-risk students. Specialized staff members, with the support of administrators, parents, and others, work closely with Re-Entry students to provide tailored curriculum, group counseling, and positive reinforcement in an effort to establish renewed identity with the educational process. In its fourth year, "Re-Entry" is a major success.

Components of the program include:

1. *Exit Conference* — student-counselor conferences which occur in proximity to a student's unsuccessful departure from school.

2. *Dropouts Invited to Return* — students are contacted in writing and/or by telephone during the summer.

3. *Mandatory Student-Parent Summer Meeting* — this orientation meeting includes discussions of alternative avenues of continuing education (adult education, military service, county programs, etc.).

4. *Personal Growth Class* — a required re-entry class wherein students earn Social Security credit. Includes monitoring of overall school performance, individual and group counseling, GGI (Guided Group

Interaction), "Grandpal" introduction, and substantive study in behavioral sciences.

5. *Recognition and Acknowledgement Activities* — breakfast out, juice and donut meetings, personal congratulative communications, etc.

6. *Exit Conferencing and Follow-up* — Re-Entry students not successful in the program are counseled as to continuance of their education, including support communication. Service likely continues with these students.

7. *Recognition and Celebration* — for students completing the school year.

Contact Person

Jim Tropea, Assistant Principal
Sterling Heights Senior High School
12901 Fifteen Mile Road
Sterling Heights, MI 48077
313-939-5900

●————————●————————●

TITLE OF PROGRAM/Curriculum

Individualized Opportunities Unlimited (IOU) (Wisconsin)

Level (High School)

Potential dropouts (Graduation Incentive Program)

Description

This program is designed to provide support in educational, vocational, and career awareness opportunities for potential school dropouts at the high-school level. Students in junior and senior classes are eligible to participate in IOU. Those students who are academically or economically disadvantaged, and who show one or more dysfunctional behaviors or attitudes that act as barriers to successful participation at school, may participate. Key criteria for participation are an inability to function properly within a regular classroom setting, a record of absenteeism and tardiness, lack of motivation and direction, behavior problems, repeated suspension and referrals to the office for discipline, and failure to establish meaningful goals for the future. IOU provides relevant classroom experience opportunities for these at-risk students. It combines regular course work, a social studies component, an employability skills class, and an opportunity to have a regular paying job in the community. School credit is awarded for successful performance on the job and in the related classes.

Contact Person

Carolyn Hughes, IOU Program Coordinator
Neenah High School
2375 Tullar Road
Neenah, WI 54956
414-729-6880

●————————●————————●

TITLE OF PROGRAM/Curriculum
Prescription Learning Lab (Colorado)

Level (High School)

Description
      PLL is a diagnostic-prescriptive multi-media instructional program for math and English. At present it is only in place at Central High School. Students are selected for the class based on poor language or math skills, low test scores, and teacher recommendation.
      Program components include:

1. One teacher and one instructional aide per class, 15 Apple computers and a mainframe computer, tape recorders and filmstrip machine, a television and a VCR, and numerous workbooks at different instructional levels.

2. Individualized instruction: students' placement test results are entered into the computer which then prescribes the level and activities which the student will pursue.

3. Small classes of no more than 15 students, thereby allowing frequent individual student contact.

4. The capability of designing the program components around each school's specific needs, goals, and requirements.

Contact Person
Kay Levinson
Central High School
1050 Newark Street
Aurora, CO 80010
303-340-1600

•———————— • ———————— •

TITLE OF PROGRAM/Curriculum
EXPO (Colorado)

Level (High School)

Description
      The purpose of the EXPO program (Experiential Program for Orientation) is to aid selected high-risk students in making the transition from middle school to high school. This transition, when coupled with the lack of socialization skills, poor self-image, and lack of interest in or fear of school situations often leads to truancies, inappropriate peer groups, poor grades, and eventually discontinuation. The program seeks to prevent problems by developing a visible support system. The program originated in Aurora Public Schools by building staff responding to an identified need.
      Unique features:

1. Students are identified and interviewed while in the eighth grade.

2. High-risk students volunteer for the program.

3. Volunteer staff and peer counselors become "sponsors" for the students during their freshman year.

Contact Person
Jeanie Johnson, Counselor
Gateway High School
1300 South Sable Boulevard
Aurora, CO 80012
303-755-7160

● ———— ● ———— ●

TITLE OF PROGRAM/Curriculum
Project 50/50 (Massachusetts)

Level   (High School)

Description
Project 50/50 is a computer technology program designed to assist secondary school students in gaining computer application skills while increasing their levels of social functioning and academic achievement. The project was developed and implemented as an education/industry partnership and has as its target population ethnic minorities, females, and disadvantaged youth.

The uniqueness of the program is found in its comprehensive approach. The curriculum focuses on computer applications and consists of four components:

• COMPUTER AS A SUBJECT covers current and future computer applications, history, terminology, and robotics

• COMPUTER AS A TOOL introduces programming in LOGO and BASIC languages and the use of graphics and word processing software

• COMPUTER AS A CAREER focuses on technology-based careers and job opportunities, job search techniques, interviewing skills, and interpersonal relations

• COMPUTER AS A METAPHOR includes exercises in orienteering, and uses map and compass skills in relation to programming a computer.

When a school adopts Project 50/50, a network with local businesses is either begun or enhanced, teachers are trained, collaboration between schools is encouraged, and a curriculum is established. In contrast to comparison groups, Project 50/50 students have demonstrated significantly greater acquisition of computer skills (as measured by the Computer Skills Test), self-esteem (as measured by the Tennessee Self-Concept Scale), and express interest in math, science, and technology (as evidenced by student schedules), based on a one-year intervention period. Following a four-year plateau of achievement scores for math, reading, and language, Project 50/50 students demonstrated significant gains compared to a norm group.

Contact Person
Michael Fields, Director
French River Teacher Center
North Oxford, MA 01537
617-987-1626

●────── ●────── ●

TITLE OF PROGRAM/Curriculum
Operation Succeed (Ohio)

Level (High School)

Description
    Operation Succeed is a program designed to: (1) encourage the student at risk of dropping out to return to school, and (2) structure in-school experiences to meet the special needs of these students so that they experience true success and obtain a diploma.
    A Management Outreach Team (MOT) Squad composed of administrators and supervisors will be organized and assigned to each of 12 comprehensive high schools and the magnet/vocational schools which serve grades 9 through 12 (CSA, Science, Law and Public Service, Aviation, Health Careers, and Max Hayes).
    Specific duties of MOT Squad members are:

1. Visit homes of assigned at-risk students.

2. Ascertain reasons for nonattendance of at-risk students.

3. Maintain ongoing personal contact with at-risk students after they have returned to school.

4. Contact assigned students who have not returned at least one month after initial contact, as follow-up.

5. Work with site staff to identify legal, health, tutorial, child care, and economic resources that are needed to meet the special needs of the at-risk students.

6. Personally provide any help to the student that is within the power of the MOT member, such as offering help with homework, providing a "sympathetic ear," etc.

7. Complete and submit on a timely basis all required forms.

8. Attend district-wide, cluster-wide, and school-level MOT vice/ meetings.

9. Initiate contact with any other at-risk students identified by the school.

10. Serve as resources to their assigned high school on an as-needed basis, such as serving as group leaders for support groups formed at the school level or identifying potential jobs.

    Each school has common resources shared system-wide as well as resources unique to its building. Basic elements considered are:

1. Flexibility in the interpretation of the attendance.

2. Restructure—The principal will identify teachers willing to work together as an instructional team to meet the specific needs of at-risk students.

3. Remedial support—The following tutorial models may be used to support remediation:
   - Peer tutoring
   - One-on-one tutoring by classroom teachers with reallocation of teaching time
   - Academic clubs
   - Volunteer tutors
   - MOT Squad members as tutors
   - Retired CPS teachers as tutors
   - University students.

4. Economic support—Economic needs are to be entered on the Student Educational Profile. Paid work experience options are available.

5. Health service—Referral to the appropriate health services will occur on a need basis. If child care services are required and available, principals will inform students of that availability.

6. Program support—The principal should ensure that suggestions and guidance concerning the type of school program a student should enroll in, as well as exploring of the options for the at-risk student, are ongoing. Channeling students into the right program is crucial to providing successful learning experiences for the at-risk student.

7. School-based support group—Support groups tailored to keep at-risk students in school shall be created by the high-school principal. These groups will meet on a regularly scheduled basis and will be comprised of at-risk students and a leader or co-leaders.

8. Student educational plan—The Student Educational Profile has been specifically designed to identify the needs of at-risk students in order to keep them in school.

Building-level staff involvement will be secured through meetings planned under the direction of the high-school principal. Existing building staff will attend to be given information about Operation Succeed.

Contact Person
Emma Benning
Cleveland Public Schools
4380 East 6th Street
Cleveland, OH 44114
216-574-8666

TITLE OF PROGRAM/Curriculum
Upward Reach (Ohio)

Level   (High School)

Description

The Upward Reach Project is designed to build upon a student's strengths and interests as well as developmental levels. The Project also encourages students to utilize youth-developing resources within the school and the community.

The Project serves approximately 1,000 students at 12 senior high schools and is aimed at those:

- Expressing dropout tendencies
- Active with Juvenile Court
- Re-entering Cleveland Public Schools from the Ohio Department of Youth Services
- Transferring back to Cleveland Public Schools from the Youth Development Center (YDC), Cuyahoga County
- Interested in motivational counseling.

The supportive services for this Project include:

- Re-entry assistance
- Individual, group sessions
- Tutoring
- Home visitations
- Referrals to school and/or community programs
- Field trips.

Special features for Upward Reach are recognition and awards, leadership training, and participation in the JOBS program.

The curriculum for the Program, which includes regular and individualized instruction along with access to supportive services, covers:

- Work-study programs
- Academic courses
- Business education courses
- Technical-vocational training.

Contact Person

Emma Benning, Assistant Superintendent
Cleveland Public Schools
4380 East 6th Street
Cleveland, OH 44114
216-574-8666

ALTERNATIVE PROGRAMS

TITLE OF PROGRAM/Alternatives
  Hellbeck Elementary Alternative (Colorado)

Level (Elementary)

Description
  Hellbeck School is operated on the concept of "Houses." Three "houses" divide students into grade-level blocks, one and two, three and four, five and six. The "house" model project at Hellbeck represents an effort to apply the best of what is known from current educational research and acknowledged good practice toward enhancing the total climate for learning in a school. Hellbeck has transformed the organizational structures within a school in the interest of personalized learning for every student. This transformation requires a rethinking of how schools might better function to meet the future needs of our children in an informational society.
  Three instructional "houses" incorporate the following essential features:

1. Multi-age grouping patterns.

2. Learning spaces redesigned to accommodate specific tasks and diverse learning styles.

3. Discipline, self-directedness, and self-paced learning.

4. Interdisciplinary learning.

5. Identification of potential talent in students as well as the development of talents already demonstrated.

6. Flexible scheduling of learning time for those experiences that meet student individual needs.

7. Staff teaming for effective program planning, instruction, evaluation, and personal professional growth.

8. Effective use of a variety of learning materials, instructional methods, and resources.

9. A humane climate with high morale and human motivation.

10. A variety of student groupings based upon specific task requirements.

11. Out-of-school learning and career orientation.

12. Distributive practice over a core curriculum.

Contact Person
  Ray Franklin
  Hellbeck Elementary School
  3000 Lakeview Avenue
  Pueblo, CO 81005
  719-564-1033

TITLE OF PROGRAM/Alternatives
  CATCH II (Oregon)

Level   (Upper Elementary through High School)

Description
    CATCH II is an alternative program for upper elementary and high school students to provide a leadership experience and/or address difficulties in school (i.e., attendance problems, disruptive, withdrawn, etc.). The program, in conjunction with student's regular school schedule, serves the child's interest and performance in the total school/social arena. The emphasis is not on specific job skills, but on general worker characteristics, and encouragement to develop personal, social, and vocational goals for the future.
    CATCH II provides direct environmental education services to middle and high school students from 11 district schools. Students typically participate in CATCH II for one or two full semesters, one full day a week. Some of the students who participate are also enrolled in one of the other districts' alternative programs. High school students may earn one off-campus credit for Environmental Science through participation in the program.

Contact Person
  Alcena Boozer, Alternative Education
    Supervisor
  Portland Public Schools
  P.O. Box 3107
  Portland, OR 97208
  503-280-5783

●────── ● ────── ●

TITLE OF PROGRAM/Alternatives
  Jeffco Open Living School (Colorado)

Level   (Preschool through 12th Grade)

Description
    The Open Education philosophy contends that children are innately motivated to explore and learn. Teachers and staff are facilitators who guide students to ensure the student's natural enthusiasm for learning is not stifled. Students learn in their own way, for their own reasons, and at their own pace. By allowing each student to follow his or her own timetable, the learning is more effective. The responsibility for learning is placed on the child with the teacher as a partner. Students have choices in subject matter and learning projects.

Preschool through Junior High:
    The students at Open Living School are part of multi-age groups: Early Learning Center (ELC), ages 5 to 8; the Intermediate (IA), ages 8 to 12; and the Junior High, ages 12 to 15. Preschool children range in age from 3 to 5. The multi-aged groups allow children to learn from each other, to be followers and, as they get older, leaders of the group. Groups also allow students and teachers to be together for three or four years.

Classroom teachers are engaged in team teaching. There is no set curriculum as in a conventional classroom. The curriculum develops as the result of teacher-team planning with input from parents and children. This allows the teachers to be both flexible and professional. The physical surroundings for the ELC children are patterned after a familiar home environment. The IA and Junior High areas are also designed to create a warmer and more personal climate for the children.

The central theme of the school is community. Parents, students, teachers, and staff comprise this community. The school is not just for the students, it is for the whole family.

The Open School (K-9) was created in 1970. In 1973, the Open Living High School began due to the success of the elementary and junior high levels.

Open High School:

The purpose of the Open High School is to provide an environment that will foster the development of the potential in each student through an emphasis on individualization and self-directed learning to prepare students for the transition from childhood to adulthood. A program has been developed to facilitate this transition through a series of passages which demonstrate a student's readiness to become an adult.

The Open High School is small for the sake of having a community where everyone is known, where no one is anonymous. The enrollment has been limited to a maximum of 235. Students are at the school by choice, as are staff members.

There is a belief that students in the school need at least one adult who knows them, cares for them, and will listen to them. Within the advisory relationship, a student and his or her advisor will develop an individualized educational program based on that student's unique strengths and needs. Advisor responsibilities include helping students set goals and determining how to reach them; monitoring accomplishments and progress in the personal, social, and intellectual domains; communicating with the home; and helping the student determine when the expectations for graduation have been met. In choosing an advisor, a student chooses an advisory group which meets weekly to discuss mutual concerns and plan activities to build group identity.

Students participate in Governancy, which convenes weekly to discuss common concerns, organize groups for action, make decisions, solve problems, reach agreements, and share in celebrations of accomplishment. There are no grades at the school, nor grade levels. Students are expected to demonstrate competence as they work toward personal goals. Self-evaluation is an ongoing process for each student. At the completion of each class or other learning experience, students write evaluations of their own performance and seek responses from their teachers or mentors.

The Walkabout Program is a feature of the program where students through various passages and activities demonstrate readiness to function as adults. Passages are begun when the advisor agrees that the student has demonstrated the ability to set meaningful goals and attain them. The triad, a small peer support group within the advisory system, may also be involved in determining readiness for the final phase of program.

Passages demonstrate the ability to apply skills in the real world. Each Passage encompasses one or more of the following areas:

1. *Adventure:* A quest, a personal meaningful challenge, the pursuit of which requires courage, endurance, self-reliance, and intelligent decisionmaking.

2. *Career Exploration:* A broad investigation of a field of employment, including an in-depth study of at least one job within that field, with particular attention to possibilities for the future.

3. *Creativity:* The development of a product that is an expression of one's personal imagination, together with a detailed analysis of the process by which it was created.

4. *Global Awareness/Volunteer Service:* The identification of an issue having global impact, followed by a study of how one's own culture and at least one other culture deal with this issue, culminating in a service project designed to influence the issue on a local level.

5. *Logical Inquiry:* An investigation which includes the generation of a hypothesis, the development of a systematic approach to data collection, and sufficient documentation to allow replication of the study.

6. *Practical Skills:* The development of proficiency in a skill or set of skills for which one was formerly dependent on others, and which has the potential for lifelong usefulness.

Contact Person
Ruth Steele, Principal
Jefferson County Open School
7655 West 10th Avenue
Lakewood, CO 80215
303-233-4878

● ———— ● ———— ●

TITLE OF PROGRAM/Alternatives
Burton International School (Michigan)

Level (Alternative, Elementary, Middle School)

Description
The Burton International School is a multi-lingual and multi-cultural school for students city-wide. Burton International School respects and supports the ethnic, racial, and cultural heritage of each of its students and plans its programs to meet their needs. It offers a balanced academic program in language arts, mathematics, social studies, science, physical education, performing arts, arts and crafts, music, and foreign language. Burton International School uses the community with its variety of ethnic and economic groups as learning resources for the children.

Burton International School encourages mutual respect and understanding among all people and expects children and adults to function in a democratic and peaceful manner. It moves toward a complete community school for all ages and groups with a cooperative and collaborative spirit between parents, teachers, and the community. All children, whatever their background, are expected to operate at their highest potential to develop an ethos of excellence.

Students will learn:

- To live together in a democratic and peaceful fashion
- To use language skills and mathematical skills effectively
- To feel good about themselves and respect each other
- How to learn and think critically
- To exercise self-discipline and set goals for themselves
- To become self-directed and develop problem solving and decision-making skills.

Contact Person

Aritha Marshall
5051 Woodward Avenue
Detroit, MI 48202
313-494-1087

●───────● ───────●

TITLE OF PROGRAM/Alternatives
Detroit Open School (Michigan)

Level (Elementary, Middle School)

Description

The Detroit Open School is a unique Detroit Public School characterized by "openness." Open educators believe children learn by exploring the real world in all its richness and variety. Open education implies an environment in which the possibilities for exploration and learning are unobstructed.

The philosophy of the Detroit Open School is directly based on the child-centered approach, fitting the individual developmental needs of each child as espoused by Piaget. The Detroit Open School encompasses all areas of growth: academic, emotional, social, physical, and aesthetic. Staff members design and fit the curriculum to the needs and interests of the child rather than the child to the curriculum. The concept is based on the premise that learning occurs most naturally during periods of intense involvement, during active-doing, and as a part of living.

Research suggests that children learn in different ways, at different times, from each other, and from things around them that interest them. The school's task is to provide individualized, flexible instruction in a personally supportive, nurturing, and happy climate. The Detroit Open School provides exciting, stimulating activities and exploratory experiences in a well-planned environment in which academic skills are important and necessary. The Detroit Open School also recognizes and encourages creative abilities.

The Detroit Open School encourages a child to learn in many directions. It encourages a child to develop talents and creative abilities, to continue learning, to be excited about new things, to be in awe and wonder of the unknown, and to become a lifelong learner. Learning is not distinguished from living, nor living from learning.

Self-direction and self-discipline, as well as the growth of a good self-concept, are encouraged and built in the program.

Contact Person
Aritha Marshall
5051 Woodward Avenue
Detroit, MI 48202
313-494-1087

•———————•———————•

TITLE OF PROGRAM/Alternatives
Eco-Seminar (Colorado)

Level (Elementary, Middle, High School)

Description
This is a semester-long class held at the Balarat Outdoor Education Center. Enrolled students are on leave from their home high school. During the semester they earn ten semester hours credit in science, ten in social studies, five in physical education and five in English. Students serve as teacher aides and research assistants. They also do site service projects that include building renovation and construction, baseline ecological studies, and trail maintenance. Typically, students teach elementary school pupils in the out-of-doors three days weekly and attend seminars on specific subjects for two days. About every third week, each student is scheduled to assist with the outdoor resident program.

Purpose: To provide enrolled students the opportunity to learn about the ecology of a mountain region, to reinforce that learning by teaching others, to enhance their human relations skills in the teaching field, to develop outdoor living skills.

Contact Person
Jim Wright
Balarat Outdoor Education Center
Denver Public Schools
1550 South Steele Street
Denver, CO 80210
303-837-1000, ext. 2678

•———————•———————•

TITLE OF PROGRAM/Alternatives
Metropolitan Learning Center (Oregon)

Level (Elementary, Middle School, High School)

Description
Metropolitan Learning Center (MLC) emphasizes positive individualized education in an open, caring environment. Students learn independence and responsible decisionmaking in a supportive setting.

The school is organized into primary, middle school, and high school programs. Cross-grade experiences permit students to grow at their own rate. Students representing each cross-section of all the grades meet in a base station for 15 minutes each day for attendance, announcements, and interpersonal skill building.

The students in the primary program spend half the day in exploratory and elective courses. Unique aspects of the program include upgraded groupings in basic skills and a strong emphasis on reading, math, and language arts skills.

The middle school section is designed to meet the unique developmental needs of the 10- to 13-year-old group.

Teachers act as counselors as well as academic advisors. Mornings are spent developing basic skills and the afternoon classes allow individual choice in classes from many elective courses.

Weekly off-campus activities enhance the students' social development. These activities encourage an understanding of social responsibility, interpersonal skills, and group dynamics.

High school students build a program to meet their own needs, abilities, interests, and learning styles. Off-campus learning experiences, in cooperation with local placement in community service organizations, are available.

Students may also elect to participate in independent study programs which can include travel or part-time employment. The high school students develop a course of study with their counselors to assure necessary credits are met for a standard or modified diploma.

Contact Person
Alcena Boozer, Alternative Education
    Supervisor
Portland Public Schools
P.O. Box 3107
Portland, OR 97208
503-280-5783

● ———— ● ———— ●

TITLE OF PROGRAM/Alternatives
Enterprise Alternative School (Michigan)

Level   (Middle School)
Eighth and ninth grade students

Description
Enterprise is a three-year program sponsored by the Comstock and Parchment School districts. It is designed to serve students who have had difficulties with achievement, attendance, and/or social relationships in the regular school setting. Students who have the potential to finish high school are selected for enrollment. The intent is to prepare students both academically and socially to enter the regular high school. Enterprise does not accept students who continually exhibit violent, aggressive, and/or hostile behavior.

Referral and Enrollment
Students are referred by teachers or counselors. Administrators must submit a referral form stating the student's history and reasons for the

referral. Forms are reviewed by the alternative school staff. Students fitting the criteria stated above are accepted. Some students are admitted on a trial basis.

Both students and parents must sign a consent form agreeing to enrollment in the program and stating that they will abide by the school's rules and policies.

Students from the Parchment and Comstock school district will receive the majority of the spots, with those from other districts being admitted on a tuition basis.

Instruction

Enterprise offers a remedial academic program, with instruction available for those who can progress at an accelerated pace. Eighth graders have classes in reading, English, math, social studies, wood shop, and physical education. Ninth grade courses include reading, English, math, science, wood shop, and physical education. Ninth graders can earn six credits which can be applied toward high school graduation requirements. Tenth grader courses include reading, English, math, geography (1 semester), general business (1 semester), wood shop, and physical education. Ninth and tenth graders can earn six credits per year which can be applied toward high school graduation requirements. A unique feature of the shop class is that students make products that are sold to the general public. Students keep approximately half of the sale price as profit, and thereby learn the basics of the free enterprise system. Additional instruction, included in course content, is done in social relationships, self-esteem, problem solving, values clarification, health education, personal money management, and similar topics.

Additional Features

Enterprise offers the following alternative education features:

1. Weekly progress reports to parents.
2. Home calls to check on absent students.
3. Close contact with juvenile court workers.
4. Small class size and frequent student-teacher interaction (approximate ratio 15/1).
5. Informal atmosphere.

Contact Person
Cam Davis, Department/Head
Enterprise Alternative School
301 North 26th Street
Comstock, MI 49041
616-388-9481

●————— ● ————— ●

TITLE OF PROGRAM/Alternatives
Alternative Education Program (Wisconsin)

Level (Middle School and High School)
Slow learners in grades 7 through 12

Description

The Alternative Program at Brookwood High School began in the 1975-76 school year. The following information should give the reader the general overview of the school district and the alternative program, including (1) the nature of the students served, (2) the objectives of the program, (3) the operational plan of the program, (4) the expected outcomes of the program, and (5) the evaluation plan used with the program.

The Norwalk-Ontario School District is a consolidated district in Southwestern Wisconsin. There are two elementary schools located in each of the district's villages and a junior-senior high located midway between the villages. Brookwood Junior High houses 81 students and Brookwood Senior High houses 143 students. The overall student/teacher ratio is 14/1.

Nature of the Students to Be Served

Students eligible for the program are slow learners in grades 7 through 12 who cannot succeed in the regular classroom when required to take all required academic subjects and when graded comparatively with the total class population. These are students who would normally be either dropouts and behavior problems or frustrated, withdrawn students allowed to pass through high school.

The criteria for placement into the alternative vocational program include:

1. An ability level within the below average range of 70 to 95 IQ.

2. An achievement level at least two grade levels below current grade placement in a majority of basic academic skills.

3. A history of failure to succeed in the classroom.

4. A probable gain from vocational courses rather than regular academic courses.

Objectives of the Program

1. To allow the slow-learning student in grades 7 through 12 to receive the proper instruction and time to master the basic skills of reading and math to his or her highest potential.

2. To provide the opportunity for slow-learning students to find success in all regular vocational courses by gaining skills supportive to the regular vocational program.

3. To provide realistic and optimistic vocational goals and plans for the slow-learning student.

4. To provide work-study opportunities for students to actually develop work and vocational skills, if possible.

5. To develop and enhance healthy behavior and social skills in students who had previously developed unhealthy patterns due to extreme lack of success in school.

While objective 4 remains a high-priority item, we have had no success in work-study endeavors over the past three years because of our limited local resources.

Operational Plan

A complete evaluation of the total school population was made during the initial year and subsequent years. Updating of this examination has included examination of group testing and teacher observation/ referral. Procedures are then followed as dictated by federal legislation (P.L. 94-142 and Section 504) and Wisconsin Statutes (5.115.80).

Through this process, the Multi-disciplinary Team and the school district then recommends placement to the parents into the Alternative Education Program. Parents must then finally give written consent for placement, and the following adjustments will be made to the student's school.

Expected Outcomes of the Program

1. Significant prevention of dropouts among slow-learning students.

2. Significant increases in reading and math abilities of slow-learning students, especially by the time of high school graduation.

3. Significant increases in knowledge and success gained by the slow-learning student in all alternative classes.

4. Significant improvement of discipline problem, introversion, and other negative behavior patterns.

5. Significant improvement in job skills and employability of the slow-learning student.

6. Significant improvement in vocational planning by slow-learning students.

7. Eventual improvement of literacy, independence behavior, and job skills of the area work force due to improved ability of the school's slow learners upon entering the world of work.

Evaluation Plan

At the time of entrance into the program, each student receives not only individual ability and achievement testing, but also personality and vocational interest evaluation by the guidance department.

Each year math, reading, and personality pre- and post-testing takes place. The math section of the Comprehensive Test of Basic skills for math, the Gates McGinitie Test for reading, and Mooney Problem's Checklist are used for personality evaluation. At the end of each year, the faculty is surveyed verbally to determine the Alternative Education Program's effect on the regular school program. This feedback from the faculty has always been positive.

Contact Person
Alan Szepi, District Administrator
Norwalk-Ontario School District
Route 1
Ontario, WI 54651
608-337-4403

TITLE OF PROGRAM/Alternatives
Fairview Alternative School (Missouri)

Level (Middle School and High School)
Students who do not function well in a traditional school setting

Description

The Fairview Alternative School is designed to serve those students who have educational or behavioral problems that hamper their success in regular school settings. Opportunities are provided for students to make necessary social adjustments and at the same time continue their progress in the academic and vocational areas.

Students are referred to the school by the district's Placement Board and by the Juvenile Court. Students may also petition the Placement Board for entry into Fairview when they feel the traditional school is not meeting their needs.

The school enrolls a maximum of 135 students from grades 8 through 12 for a minimum of one school year. (The number of grade eight students is limited.) A staff of 15 includes the following teachers: special reading, special education, EMH, LD, and two BD. The basic curriculum consists of English, math, science, social studies, art, physical education, homemaking, engine repair, and business education.

A Screening, Assignment, and Evaluation (SAE) Committee meets, examines each student's records and the nature of the problem, and interviews the student to determine his or her academic and vocational preferences. The committee draws up an individual education plan for each student, which both the student and parent sign. The committee is composed of the principal, counselor, home school coordinator, psychological examiner, and psychiatrist and/or clinical psychologist, when appropriate.

Contact Person
Curtis Rogers, Principal
Fairview Alternative School
3850 Pittman Road
Kansas City, MO 64133
816-353-1258

●──────● ──────●

TITLE OF PROGRAM/Alternatives
Flint Schools of Choice (Michigan)

Level (Middle School and High School)
Junior and senior high school students (Grades 7 through 12)

Description

An alternative education program designed to reach students who experience difficulty in a traditional school setting. The Flint Schools of Choice is actually three schools within a school: Alternative High School for the 10th through 12th grades, Alternative Junior High School for 7th through 9th, and Continuation School for pregnant girls of junior and senior high school age.

A contract method of instruction is used at the Alternative High School. All Flint High School students are eligible to enroll, and promotion and graduation requirements meet district standards.

Students with behavior and attendance problems are referred to the Alternative Junior High School and receive comprehensive counseling services in addition to uniquely tailored academic course work.

The Continuation School provides programs and services for girls who want to continue their education during pregnancy. In addition to regular courses, there is instruction in prenatal care, preparation for labor and delivery, nutrition and child care. An on-site nursery provides infant care while mothers attend their classes.

Contact Person
Edward Thorne, Principal
Flint Schools of Choice
517 Fifth Avenue
Flint, MI 48502
313-762-1390

●————— ● ————— ●

TITLE OF PROGRAM/Alternatives
Port Huron Alternative Learning Center (Michigan)

Level　(Middle School and High School)
12- to 17-year-old disenchanted youths who have failed to function in the normal school setting

Description
The Port Huron Alternative Learning Center (PHALC) is a school for disenchanted youths who cannot function in the traditional school setting for reasons of truancy, poor academic performance, and/or behavioral problems. Our purpose is to provide students with the opportunity to continue their education while attempting to modify their unacceptable behavior. The ultimate goal of both staff and students is to return the students to their home-base school and have them function successfully.

Students are referred for admission to PHALC by their home-base schools. Once approved, the students are tested and enrolled in classes in which they are taught on an individual basis. The subjects offered are equivalent to courses taught in the school districts' intermediate and high schools. Students are evaluated every six weeks by a pass/fail grading system. Course credits are issued each semester and can be applied toward a high school diploma.

Port Huron Alternative Learning Center has grown from a part-time program of 60 students and 3 staff to a full-time program with 300 students staffed by 30 certified and service personnel. The 1988-89 school year is our 11th year of operation, and we attribute our continued growth and success to the philosophy that all students do not learn at the same time nor in the same way.

The Family Life Education Center (FLEC) is an alternative high school for pregnant and parenting teens. The goal of the FLEC program is to enable the teen parent to complete her high school education. Students enroll in high school completion classes and classes in Teen Pregnancy, Parenting, and Nursery Aide. Childbirth preparation classes are taught by a registered nurse. Individual counseling is provided by a certified social worker. Free child care is available in an on-site licensed nursery.

Contact Person
Mr. Joseph P. Martindale
Port Huron Area School District
3001 Electric Avenue
Port Huron, MI 48060
313-984-6561

● ————— ● ————— ●

TITLE OF PROGRAM/Alternatives
Stockbridge High School (Michigan)

Level (Middle and High School)
Students in grades 7 through 12 who have poor attendance patterns

Description
Students in grades 7 through 12 who have gotten behind in school, are in trouble in school, or have truancy problems.

Students are referred by their base high schools to the District's Student Services' office. This office officially makes the transfer of students to Stockbridge High School.

Stockbridge is housed on the third floor of an old building, once used as a high school. It has a capacity of 300 students at present and can be expanded to accommodate more students should the need arise.

An individualized "learning center" approach is the basis of our educational delivery system. We make use of both a "time out" (in-house suspension) room and a "break room." Each teacher has a "check book" and writes out a check every Friday for perfect attendance and for a student completing a credit. The checks may be used like cash in our "break room" and even to buy days off. Teachers teach six of eight class periods. Each class is 50 minutes long.

Contact Person
Russ Harmelink, Principal
Stockbridge High School
Grand Rapids Public Schools
615 Turner, N.W.
Grand Rapids, MI 49504
616-984-6561

● ————— ● ————— ●

TITLE OF PROGRAM/Alternatives
Media Academy (California)

Level (High School)

Description
Fremont High School has established a school within a school aimed at students at risk, focusing particularly on increasing the engagement of black and Hispanic students at risk. This three-year program includes exposure to occupations in media such as journalism, newspapers, radio, and television. Classes in English, math, science, and social studies are taken daily, in addition to a two-block period and lab for media activities. Academics are taught through communication orientation.

Students find this approach motivating in that they find intrinsic rewards through being in the area (media) in which they are most interested. The program allows students a sense of ownership.

Contact Person
Steve O'Donoghue
Fremont High School
Oakland Unified School District
Oakland, CA 94612
415-261-3240

● —————— ● —————— ●

TITLE OF PROGRAM/Alternatives
Vocational Village High School (Oregon)

Level (High School)

Description
Vocational Village serves students who have dropped out of regular school programs and whose needs are not well met in traditional classroom settings. Vocational Village offers both academic and vocational coursework. Eight career clusters are offered: food service, electronics, industrial mechanics, health services, marketing, office occupations, graphic arts, and welding/sheet metal. An evening sequence is also offered. Some students are referred by the home high schools, courts, or from special education programs. It utilizes a former business site in Southeast Portland.

Contact Person
Alcena Boozer, Alternative Education
    Supervisor
P.O. Box 3107
Portland, OR 97208
503-280-5783

● —————— ● —————— ●

TITLE OF PROGRAM/Alternatives
Wilson Alternative (Oregon)

Level (High School)

Description
Students spend half a day in the regular program, and half a day at the Mary Tieke School site campus. Students who enter the Wilson alternative are freshmen or sophomores who have difficulty adjusting to the

school's mod-flex scheduling and require a more structured academic setting, freshmen who are failing their core classes because of poor attendance, freshmen from alternatives elsewhere, or sophomores who earned no freshman credit in their core classes. The program offers English, general math, introduction to algebra, and global studies. Students who participate in the morning take three classes and afternoon participants take four classes.

Students are characterized as low in self-esteem, distrustful of teachers and authority figures, impatient with regular school routine, lacking motivation and organization and time management skills, and may have behavioral problems as well as personal problems such as substance abuse and nonsupportive home situations. The goal of the program is to mainstream performance.

Contact Person
Alcena Boozer, Alternative Education
    Supervisor
Portland Public Schools
P.O. Box 3107
Portland, OR 97208
503-280-5783

● ————— ● ————— ●

TITLE OF PROGRAM/Alternatives
Whitaker Alternative (Oregon)

Level (High School)

Description
Whitaker Alternative is a self-contained alternative program designed to develop positive learning attitudes before absenteeism, negative attitudes, and poor academic performance become permanent behavior patterns.

Each unit of study focuses on developing a sense of responsibility and belonging in an atmosphere of excitement, challenge, and success. Basic skills (reading, writing, and English) are incorporated into courses such as marine biology, horticulture, and animal studies. Math is taken within the regular school setting. Students are involved in choosing their learning experiences; staff work with them in this process. Students also participate in group counseling.

Students in the alternative school typically attend full time. Course offerings of the Whitaker program include social studies, science and art, language arts, reading, math, and Sustained Silent Reading/Study.

Contact Person
Alcena Boozer, Alternative Education
    Supervisor
Portland Public Schools
P.O. Box 3107
Portland, OR 97208
503-280-5783

● ————— ● ————— ●

TITLE OF PROGRAM/Alternatives
Northwest Alternative Center (Colorado)

Level   (High School)

Description
This is an off-campus alternative special education program serving students identified as having emotional and behavioral disorders so severe that they cannot be maintained or effectively educated in the District's most restrictive high school emotional/behavioral disorder programs. The program also serves as a provisional placement for students returning to the District from either residential or day treatment programs as a transition to less restrictive programs, when appropriate.

This program offers a basic academic curriculum, some electives, vocational exploration, supervised work experience, and ongoing treatment services to both students and their families. The goal is to return students to less restrictive school programs when possible, with staff assistance in re-entry planning and follow-up. For students not returning to other school programs, goals are established for effective integration into vocational or other community placements.

Contact Person
Marian Fagerstrom, Special Education
   Coordinator
Aurora Public Schools
11023 East Fifth Avenue
Aurora, CO 80010
303-340-0510

• ———— • ———— •

TITLE OF PROGRAM/Alternatives
Alternative Center for Education (ACE) (Colorado)

Level   (High School)

Description
ACE serves 150 students with a staff of nine full-time teachers, four part-time teachers, a half-time social worker, one secretary, and one administrator. The program is an extension of the two traditional high schools. Students must apply through their home high school. A waiting list is maintained. Home school counselors and administrators prioritize students on the waiting list. The alternative program requires a parent and student orientation group meeting and an individual interview prior to admission.

Class size is 15 to 18 students. District curriculum objectives are followed; students graduate with a home high school diploma. Students take four to seven classes. Attendance and achievement are based on a contract system. Failure to complete a contract results in probation and waiver (suspension) status.

Grading, contract, probation, and waiver periods are 18 days. There are five 18-day periods in a semester. One semester hour of credit may be earned for passing a class each 18-day period.

Contact Person
Jeanne Hartfelder, Administrator
Alternative Center for Education
3455 West 72nd Avenue
Westminster, CO 80030
303-428-2575

•————— •————— •

TITLE OF PROGRAM/Alternatives
Alternative High School (Colorado)

Level (High School)

Description
Small group instruction: individualized contracting; flexible scheduling; full academic course work; career exploration; community exploration, work-study; credit system based on earning 75 clock hours per 1/2 Carnegie unit; nongraded, student-governed program; weekly monitored student progress, mailed to parents as requested or teacher-parent-student meeting. Telephone conferences as needed, weekly credit checks for progress for all students. Counselor available at all times. Computer-assisted classes in math, language arts, and social studies. At least two parent/student/teacher conferences yearly.

Staff Size: Nine

Funding Source: School district budgeted

School District Sponsoring Agency: Adams County District 1

Hours of Operation: 7:45 a.m.-2:30 p.m. (Students)
7:15 a.m.-2:45 p.m. (Teacher)

School Structure: Autonomous

Target Population: Dropouts; dropout-prone; difficulty in succeeding in traditional school system.

Contact Person
Don C. Cost, Principal
Alternative #1 High School
1200 East 78th Avenue
Denver, CO 80229
303-287-9400

•————— •————— •

TITLE OF PROGRAM/Alternatives
High School Redirection (Colorado)

Level (High School)
Grades 9-12

Description
High School Redirection is a new four-year, diploma-granting, alternative high school. It is a school of choice that emphasizes affective and experiential learning. The curriculum includes an advisement program,

interdisciplinary classes, and an intensive reading program. Field trips and community service provide students with hands-on experiences.

Unique to the school is a child care center where teen parents may leave their children while they attend classes. In addition, the center provides parenting skills classes and volunteer opportunities to explore child care as a career.

The school is currently exploring alternative methods of assessing progress and granting a diploma based on exhibition of skills and learning outcomes. This proposal will be developed by January, 1990. The ultimate goal of the school is to enable students to become lifelong learners.

A grant from the United States Department of Labor through Denver Employment and Training Administration has paid a portion of the costs for the first and second year. The balance is paid for by the Denver Public Schools. The district will make a decision about fully funding the school by the third year.

During the first year, a major portion of the enrollment were at-risk youth. The most dramatic changes in these students have been behavioral and attitudinal. It is expected that these students will now focus their energies on goal setting and individualized learning outcomes during the second year of the school.

Contact Person
Pauline McBeth
1900 Downing Street
Denver, CO 80218
303-860-9586

• ———— • ———— •

TITLE OF PROGRAM/Alternatives
Southwest Open High School (Colorado)

Level (High School)

Description
Southwest Open High School (SWOHS) is a second-chance program under the Southwest Board of Cooperative Services offering students in four school districts — Montezuma-Cortez, Dolores, Mancos, and Dove Creek — an alternative approach in public education. SWOHS each year serves 50 to 120 students with extremely diverse needs, both academically and personally. SWOHS serves several at-risk student groups including pregnant teens, adjudicated youth, Native Americans, teen parents, part-time and full-time working teens, and students from single parent and dysfunctional families. Thus, the school has established a system of individualized educational planning with each student. Each student is assigned an advisor who as both a teacher and counselor coordinates the student's learning program. Advisors encourage students to direct their learning experiences most appropriate to their interests and learning styles. In this process students write Passages, which outline what learning they wish to accomplish and how they will achieve their listed personal, social, and academic goals. Students are involved in creative and meaningful Passages such as volunteerism in community programs, internships

with area business, outdoor challenges, field studies, and other out-of-classroom experiences. In addition, students are challenged to teach classes in subjects they excel in to foster the concept of peer teaching. The staff offers high-interest activities and interdisciplinary courses on current events and relevant topics which students can incorporate into their Passages. Weekly class schedules and individual educational plans are developed and discussed during Governance, the all-school meetings each Monday morning. During Governance, students and staff are free to bring up conflicts on school issues, classes they would like to see or offer, and Passages that have been completed. Community members and parents are also invited to Governance to provide input and observe school processes. In conclusion, students and staff try to create a more personalized as well as holistic approach to education.

Contact Person
Richard Fulton, Director
P.O. Box 1420
Cortez, CO 81321
303-565-1150

●——————— ● ——————— ●

TITLE OF PROGRAM/Alternatives
Alternative and Continuing Education Program
(California)

Level (High School)

Description
The Alternative and Continuing Education Program offers various programs for students to complete their high school diploma at their own individual pace in a manner which is consistent with their life roles. Students who are employed can complete their high school diploma through independent study contracts. Students who are 16 to 18 years old who are unable to adjust to the comprehensive high school setting may enroll in the Continuation High School. For 14- to 16-year-old youths, Opportunity Classes are available to prevent high-risk youth from dropping out of school.

The program also addresses young adults who have a need to learn English and improve basic literacy skills. These young people are potential dropouts. Each program has its own counseling component to help direct students in an educational mode that best fits their needs. Classes are strategically located throughout the communities served by the district, and class schedules run from early morning to late evening to accommodate special needs. Close cooperation with JTPA strengthens program offerings and student opportunities to combine classroom work with valuable vocational training.

Contact Person
> Jean Klinghoffer, Coordinator
> Alternative and Continuing Education
> Fullerton Union High School District
> 780 Beechwood Avenue
> Fullerton, CA 92635
> 714-671-4352

• ———— • ———— •

TITLE OF PROGRAM/Alternatives
> Career Opportunity Center (Kansas)

Level (High School)

Description
> The Career Opportunity Center is a year-round alternative school designed to assist high school dropouts, 16 years and older, in earning a high school diploma or preparing for the GED certificate. The Career Opportunity Center operates on an open-entry, open-exit system. There are no classes per se and all coursework is designed and taught on an individualized, one-to-one basis. There are no attendance requirements, although students are encouraged to discuss with each of their instructors their progress in each of their courses every week. Courses do not operate on a certain number of hours for credit but are designed to be task-completion or competency based. A contract stating the material to be covered, the tasks to be completed, and the competency to be reached is signed by both the instructor and the student. There are no grades.
> Credit is earned when contracts are completed. Many of the courses are based on the Adult Performance Level (APL) theory of literacy.

Contact Person
> Carolyn Conklin, Director
> Career Opportunity Center
> 2542 Junction Road
> Kansas City, KS 66106
> 913-262-2536

• ———— • ———— •

TITLE OF PROGRAM/Alternatives
> New Directions High School (Florida)

Level (High School)

Description
> New Directions is a voluntary, alternative high school for students whose learning styles have impeded them from experiencing success in traditional high school settings. The program emphasizes an individualized self-paced curriculum that conforms to individual learning rates and styles. Students attend academic classes for one half day. Students spend

the remainder of the day attending vocational school, doing volunteer work, or at a part-time job. Students who are 15 or older and have finished the eighth grade may apply to New Directions. Acceptance of a student occurs only after the parents, student, and principal meet and discuss the program.

The New Directions curriculum consists of a full range of high school courses for required and elective credit. Credits are awarded upon demonstration of mastery of student performance standards. Credit may be earned prior to a student having spent 135 hours of in-class study. Most elective courses consist of employability skills, work experience, and vocational courses. All students attending New Directions must either take vocational courses, work part time in a supervised work-study program, or do supervised volunteer work.

The IDEAL School in Sarasota County offers a similar program to students in the southern part of the country.

Contact Person
Diane Eubanks, Principal
4409 Sawyer Road
Sarasota, FL 33583
813-923-4915

● ———— ● ———— ●

TITLE OF PROGRAM/Alternatives
Alternative Academic Skill-Building Program (California)

Level (High School)

Description
In existence since 1973, the Oakland Street Academy is an alternative storefront school for students who have left the public school system for various reasons without earning a high school diploma. It incorporates personalized guidance and teaching, using community-oriented teachers. The hours are from 9:00 a.m. to noon, and 130 students attend. Emphasis is on job skills and attitudes and/or college preparation. Students can attend staff meetings and share in the decisionmaking. Entering students' competencies are evaluated, and progress is rated on that basis, with students moving at their own speed. The program was designated a Noteworthy Practice by the State Department of Education.

Contact Person
Pat Williams, Principal
Oakland Street Academy
1449 Miller Street
Oakland, CA 94601
415-532-7556

● ———— ● ———— ●

TITLE OF PROGRAM/Alternatives
Apollo Program (California)

Level (High School)

Description
The Apollo Program is designed as a school-within-a-school for unmotivated and problem students who might otherwise not receive an education. It is characterized by a relaxed environment, a minimum of teacher authority, and individual attention. Students decide how many units they will complete. The program was designated a Noteworthy Practice by the State Department of Education.

Contact Person
Stan O'Hara
North High School
300 Galaxy Avenue
Bakersfield, CA 93308
805-399-3351

TITLE OF PROGRAM/Alternatives
Peninsula Academies (California)

Level (High School)

Description
Students involved in the academy concept begin in the 10th grade and continue through the 12th grade. They are enrolled in a core academic school-within-a-school program consisting of English, math, science, and a laboratory class related to specific occupations. During the remainder of the day they participate in regular school activities. The program has an exceptionally strong school/business partnership geared to existing job markets. Twenty academies have been established in California covering health services, computers and electronics, agriculture, hotel and restaurant occupations, and business/banking skills. Results of a thorough evaluation, replication guide, video tapes, and brochures are available at a minimal cost.

Menlo-Atherton High School focuses on computer technology. Sequoia High School's academy program is electronics oriented. Both programs accommodate up to 200 students each, beginning in 10th grade.

Contact Person
Mr. Bill Vines
Peninsula Academies
Sequoia Union High School District
480 James Street
Redwood City, CA 94062
415-369-1411

TITLE OF PROGRAM/Alternatives
School to Open Possibilities (California)

Level (High School)

Description

This program offers a successful alternative to traditional schools by utilizing independent study and contract instruction methods to meet the needs of students. Student assessment is a vital component leading to the development of pre-employment skills and to the securing of a high school diploma or its equivalent.

Contact Person

Mr. Karl Modgling
or Mr. Jack Rudd
Ceres Unified School District
P.O. Box 307
Ceres, CA 95307
209-537-4717 or 209-538-0150

● ——————— ● ——————— ●

TITLE OF PROGRAM/Alternatives
Kearsley Alternative Education Program (Michigan)

Level (High School)
Anyone 14 years of age up to age 18 who is not attending regular day classes

Description

Design

1. The alternative education program is basically an attempt to try something different to increase the chances that school will be relatively stable, orderly, humane, and a satisfying place to spend the day.

2. The program is designed for young people who are unsuccessful— academically or socially—in the public school system and to aid the student in achieving a successful re-entry into the public school system.

Referral

1. Students may be referred to the program screening committee by a teacher, counselor, principal, or attendance office.

2. The committee accepts or declines the student's application after an interview with the program director, the student, and his or her parent or guardian.

Instruction

1. Classes consist of two 17-week semesters.

2. All classes are governed course outlines.

3. All students may take classes in math, English, history, and science, with some electives offered.

Contact Person
Mr. Terry Dawson
Kearsley Community Services
The Paro Educational Center
5340 North Genesse Road
Flint, MI 48506
313-736-0990

● ——— ● ——— ●

TITLE OF PROGRAM/Alternatives
Swartz Creek Community Schools Community Education,
School of Choice (Michigan)

Level (High School)
Grades 9 through 12, students who exhibit one or more of the following: inability to function properly within the traditional classroom; academic skill development below ability level; general recognition as an under-achiever; a pattern of behavior problems, absenteeism, and tardiness

Description
The goals and objectives of the School of Choice are to reduce the alienation and improve the self-image of the student, with the expectation of obtaining the following: attitude toward school will improve for students; interaction of student with peers, parents, and adults will show improvement; attitude of parents of the students toward school will improve; the involvement of parents of students with the school will increase; academic achievement for the group will improve; grade point average of students will be enhanced; attendance will improve; tardiness will decrease; discipline referrals will be reduced; school suspensions will decrease; number of dropouts will decline.

This Center is housed outside the regular high school and stresses flexible student scheduling, i.e., the student may combine schooling and a job. The Center is open mornings, afternoons, and evenings for maximum individualized programming for each student.

The School of Choice concept was created to expand the opportunities for education to those who are least educated and most in need of education. Typically, these students are between the ages of 15 to 18 years, and have accumulated very few credits in the regular high school setting. Often compounding their learning problems are lack of reading skills and, for some, psychosocial maladjustment.

With its emphasis on appropriate instructional programs and a reading lab staffed by a reading specialist, the School of Choice is a resource center where a student may learn not only the basics, but may also identify possible careers and gain life experience in holding a job, either full- or part-time. Essentially, the community is the classroom. The student may have the option of attending the regular high school or the Skill Center for part of each day. Each student's needs are the priority in the School of Choice.

Contact Person
Gary A. Huffman, Director Community
   Education
8197 Miller Road
Swartz Creek, MI 48473
313-635-4441

• —————— • —————— •

TITLE OF PROGRAM/Alternatives
Alternative Programs (Oregon)

Level   (High School)

Description
Emphasis is placed on retention and helping students solve problems relating to their academic, social, or environmental needs. The program is located within Cleveland High School and is designed for students with varied scholastic skills who are not benefiting from the regularly structured system.

Students are placed in Option classes which correspond to their problem areas. These classes are in addition to regular scheduled courses. Freshmen and sophomores may take courses in the basics of math, English, and social studies, while juniors and seniors enroll in U.S. history, English, economics, and career courses. All classes apply toward graduation credits.

Qualified juniors and seniors may also enroll in the Career Awareness Related Education (CARE) program. This is an experience-based career exploration which enables the students to be involved in both the business community and the classroom.

Students are responsible for several short explorations, one in-depth exploration, and academic assignments for their grade. This combination enables students to achieve credits in any of three required content areas, or elective credit towards graduation.

Contact Person
Alcena Boozer, Alternative Education
   Supervisor
Portland Public Schools
P.O. Box 3107
Portland, OR 97208
503-280-5783

• —————— • —————— •

TITLE OF PROGRAM/Alternatives
Focus Program (Oregon)

Level   (High School)

Description
Special individualized projects are used to assist students who need help in basic skills or need a small, secure learning setting and structure. This program within Madison High School is geared toward students with

attendance, behavioral, and other problems which interrupt the regular learning procedure. Learning and behavioral contracts between students and teachers are used when necessary.

Students receive counseling on school and family problems from four Focus teachers and the regular Madison counseling staff.

Basic skills instruction, closely monitored attendance, and independent studies are incorporated to help students meet requirements for a standard diploma.

Conferences and written evaluations of work occur each month and parents receive a report on the student's progress. Students earn a pass/no pass grade, and recommendations by teachers on future classes are given.

On-the-job training is offered through the Practical Application of Career Application (PACE) program. Students choose a career area of interest and employers are contacted. Once an agreement is reached, the training begins.

A self-study program also is available. Students work on packets of different topics and a test is given when they are completed. Both of these programs give the students responsibility and boost self-confidence.

If students desire, other classes within Madison's regular schedule may be taken in addition to Focus courses.

Contact Person
Alcena Boozer, Alternative Education
    Supervisor
Portland Public Schools
P.O. Box 3107
Portland, OR 97208
503-280-5783

● ———— ● ———— ●

TITLE OF PROGRAM/Alternatives
Evening High (Oregon)

Level   (High School)

Description
This program provides an opportunity for temporarily or permanently excused students to seek further education or to earn additional credits toward graduation at their day school. All classes offered fulfill district and state requirements for a standard diploma.

The goals of the program are to increase achievement in basic skills and to foster human relations. Emphasis is placed on recognizing the importance and worth of an individual. An environment is created in which students can develop positive behavior patterns.

Students who attend the night school are divided into three groups instead of the traditional freshman, sophomore, junior, and senior.

Contact Person
Alcena Boozer, Alternative Education
    Supervisor
Portland Public Schools
P.O. Box 3107
Portland, OR 97208
503-280-5783

● ————●————●

TITLE OF PROGRAM/Alternatives
High School Academies (New York)

Level (High School)

Description
    The high school academies are three-year schools-within-a-school, offering economically disadvantaged students an integrated academic-vocational education, career development and enrichment activities, extensive academic and nonacademic supports, and employment opportunities. They are the joint efforts of school districts, local business and industry, and an intermediary agency—usually community-based—such as the Urban League. The academies make the educational experience of students more relevant by linking course work to employment opportunities in a local business or industry and help them make a successful transition to work or postsecondary education.
    Academies have been in existence for 20 years in Philadelphia where there are currently 11 academies enrolling 1,350 students. Academies have also been established in Portland, Oregon, Pittsburgh, Pennsylvania, and California, where there are 18 academies offering a variety of vocational fields, including business, health, computers, electronics, and building trades. The academies are one of the few dropout-prevention programs that has been evaluated systematically. The evidence is that the academy program decreases dropout rates, enhances student achievement, and increases rates of postgraduation employment and education. Academies have received numerous commendations from educators and business. Public/Private Ventures has called the academy the "best single model in the country for business involvement in the schools."
    Partnerships for Learning: School Completion and Employment Preparation in the High School Academies, a source book to help interested educators, advocates, and industry representatives establish high school academies as part of their dropout prevention interventions, is available from the Academy for Educational Development, 100 Fifth Avenue, New York, NY 10011, (212) 243-1110.

Contact Person
Hayes Mizell
Edna McConnell Clark Foundation
250 Park Avenue
New York, NY 10017
212-986-7050

● ————●————●

TITLE OF PROGRAM/Alternatives
City-As-School (CAS) (New York)

Level (High School)

Description

CAS is an alternative high school which links students with learning experiences of a business, civic, cultural, political, or social nature throughout any size community. It has been validated by JDRP as an effective program for high-risk youth. The underlying concept is that the world of experience can be joined with the world of learning, thereby making school more relevant for those students who find the traditional school setting threatening or unrelated to their present and future plans, or who seek new educational experiences. Instead of attending classes in one building, students move from learning experience to learning experience and receive academic credit for each learning experience successfully completed. Teachers are divided into Resource Coordinators and Teacher Advisors. Each Teacher Advisor holds weekly orientations, seminars, and class meetings, and is responsible for individual meetings with student and/or parents as well as for writing college evaluations. Resource Coordinators are responsible for developing new community site placement and developing the curriculum for each site. Regular visits to learning sites are required.

Contact Person
Joan McLachlan Douglas
City-As-School
16 Clarkson Street
New York, NY 10014
212-691-7801

TITLE OF PROGRAM/Alternatives
Comprehensive Competencies Program (CCP) (Colorado)

Level (High School, Adult)

Description

CCP is a North Central Accredited high school program that is competency based, open entry/open exit, and a self-paced individualized program within a learning laboratory setting. The lab is located at a non-school site and contains a variety of instructional materials, including computer-assisted instruction and audiovisual materials. Some of the unique qualities of the lab: (1) allows for each learner to work on what is needed at a pace which is comfortable; (2) permits flexible scheduling to accommodate individual situations; (3) offers instructional options to meet each learner's needs and learning styles; (4) provides frequent feedback on progress and maintains accountability for learning efforts and outcomes; (5) enhances learner efficacy by giving learners responsibility and choice; (6) maximizes applied learning time or time on task; (7) provides one-on-one attention and assistance when needed.

Lab time is available mornings, afternoons, evenings, and Saturday mornings.

Referrals of potential dropouts or high-risk youth are made by high school counselors. Eligibility requirements for youth are:

1. The lab is open to only juniors and seniors, or ages 16 to 21.

2. Students must provide for their own transportation.

3. A maximum of 1 credit total can be attained for high school credit. No more than 1/2 credit is available in any subject area.

4. In addition to the above requirements, students who are in danger of dropping out of school must meet two or more of the following Job Training Partnership Act (JTPA) high-risk indicators:

   a. He/she is a member of a family (or is a family of one) living at or below the poverty level (i.e., meets JTPA eligibility criteria);

   b. He/she has a poor attendance record (frequent absences, tardiness, truancy);

   c. He/she has a poor academic record, including failure to advance to the next grade;

   d. He/she has significant deficiencies in computing (math), reading, or writing;

   e. He/she has insufficient credits for graduation in his/her senior year;

   f. He/she has documented emotional/behavioral problems which may result in suspension (e.g., delinquency, immature behavior for grade level, drug/alcohol abuse, weak social skills);

   g. He/she is a teen parent and/or a pregnant girl;

   h. He/she has formerly dropped out and returned to high school.

Students can work toward a GED, a diploma from the Aurora Public Schools Adult Evening High School Program, or transfer CCP credit to their home high school. These classes can be applied to graduation requirements in their respective high school programs. Students are tested upon entry into the program and progress is monitored regularly with immediate feedback to each student. The program is sponsored through Arapahoe and Adams County Employment and Training which receives funding through the federally mandated JTPA sources.

Contact Person
Harry Chan
9859 East 16th Avenue
Aurora, CO 80010
303-366-4417
303-344-8060, ext. 253

TITLE OF PROGRAM/Alternatives
Olde Columbine Alternative Education (Colorado)

Level (High School, Adult)

Description
Olde Columbine High School, located in Longmont, Colorado, is specifically designed to work with alternative, at-risk youth who want to attain a St. Vrain Valley School District diploma. Enrollment is approximately 85 students who have passed the eighth grade level and are age 16 or above.

Our "Open Door" program is a retrieval program which allows students to earn credit in math and English while they focus on career choices and educational goals. Most of these students eventually try to enroll in Olde Columbine High School.

Our Adult Basic Education program includes English as a Second Language, Amnesty, GED preparation, and high school completion as components.

Finally, Teen Parenting works with young women up to age 20 who are pregnant, or have children up to 6 months in age, who want to continue their high school education.

Contact Person
William R. Blick, Principal
Olde Columbine Alternative School
621 Baker Street
Longmont, CO 80501
303-772-6161

TITLE OF PROGRAM/Alternatives
GED (Colorado)

Level (Adult)

Description
The General Educational Development program provides opportunities for high school dropouts to earn a high school equivalency diploma — a credential recognized as a key to employment opportunities, advancement, further education, and financial awards.

There are two components of the GED program. The first is a preparation class that provides direct instruction in all academic areas contained within the GED test. These areas include essay writing skills, social studies, science, reading skills, and mathematics. Upon appropriate academic preparation in each of these areas, students are encouraged to register to take the GED test. Once the student has successfully passed each of the tests, he or she is awarded a GED certificate.

Nearly 95 percent of all colleges admit GED graduates on the same basis as traditional high school graduates. The GED program is sponsored by the American Council on Education and set by the National Association of Secondary School Principals.

The GED Preparation and Testing Program is offered through Aurora Public Schools Adult and Community Education.

Contact Person
Kathy Kirkpatrick, Ed.D., Director
Continuing Education
Aurora Public Schools
1085 Peoria
Aurora, CO 80011
303-344-8060, ext. 253

• ———— • ———— •

TITLE OF PROGRAM/Alternatives
Remediation and Training Institute (D.C.)

Level (Adult)

Description
This is the seventh year of a project funded by the Ford Foundation, named the *Comprehensive Competencies Program*, a competency based instructional program in basic academic and functional skills. About 400 "Learning Centers" are now using the system, which includes a matrix of thousands of lessons. Diagnostic screening tests are administered, E by McGraw Hill, which has three levels, one to five, six to eight, and nine to GED. Students are then placed where skills need to be attained; they progress to the next skill after a series of five to eight lessons and post-testing, if the skill has been mastered. Students also learn how to use books, software, and video equipment related to lessons.

Each Learning Center pays $1,000 a year to belong to the network. Evaluative data are sent by the Learning Centers to U.S. Basics Skills Investment Corp. on a quarterly basis, and "reviews" by U.S. Basics are fed back to the sites each quarter. The cost for setting up a full program, including instructional materials, computers, software, and video equipment, ranges from $30,000 to $50,000. Centers have the capacity to serve 25 to 50 learners in each session, or hundreds per week. The ingredients of the program include:

- Individualized Instruction: Each learner can work at whatever pace is comfortable

- Competency-Based Education: Accommodate individual situations as rapidly as mastery is achieved

- Instructional Options: Different materials and media easily accessible to address instructional objectives so each learner's needs and learning style can be accommodated

- Self-Directed Learning: Learners are given responsibility, choice, and a substantial degree of control, enhancing their feeling of efficacy and their commitment

- Positive Reinforcement: Instruction in easily mastered steps, and frequent mastery tests documenting progress, provide recognition and reinforcement for learning achievements

- Accountability: Frequent feedback on the status of each learner so problems can be identified and addressed

- Maximum Time on Task: Each learner works individually on appropriate materials, with little time lost to group disruptions or explanations

- One-on-One Attention: Teachers and aides have the time and tools to provide one-on-one attention and assistance when needed

- Supportive Environment: Participant's learning or outside problems can be addressed without disrupting other learners

- Work and Training Linkages: With flexible scheduling, learning can be more easily linked with work, training, and education activities.

Contact Person
John Smith, Program Development Manager
U.S. Basic Skills Investment Corp.
1700 Diagonal Road, Suite 400
Alexandria, VA 22314
703-684-1265

●————————— ● ——————— ●

TITLE OF PROGRAM/Alternatives
CCP English as a Second Language (CCP ESL) (Virginia)

Level (Adult)

Description
     CCP ESL is a complete, individualized, self-paced, competency based program specifically designed to meet the needs of learners with limited English proficiency. Based on the principles which make CCP so successful, it is available as an add-on to CCP or as a stand-alone instructional system. This integrated, multi-media curriculum stresses listening and speaking as well as reading and writing skills, beginning at the most elementary academic and functional levels.
     The cost for setting up a full program, including instructional materials, computers, software, and video equipment, ranges from $8,000 to $30,000, depending on the equipment ordered.
     The ingredients of the program include:

- 240 CCP ESL lesson binders for Academic and functional ESL

- Core Print Materials with Audio Cassettes

- References to the most popular commercially available print materials and CAI

- Tutor-based activities, totalling 268 activities

- A sequenced set of over 3,000 language cards corresponding to all lessons

- CCP Supplementary Materials Starter Set consisting of selected commercial ESL print materials from a variety of publishers

- CCP Lesson Arrangements Kit with separate binders for Academic and Functional ESL

- 10 CCP Mastery Test binders including all subject, level, and unit tests for Academic and Functional ESL

- Audiovisual equipment, including audio cassette players and CCP Language Card Readers with head sets

Contact Person

Andreas Achilla, Special Projects Team Coordinator
U.S. Basic Skills Investment Corp.
1700 Diagonal Road, Suite 400
Alexandria, VA 22314
703-684-1265

• ———— • ———— •

TITLE OF PROGRAM/Alternatives
CCP Citizenship Competencies Program (Virginia)

Level (Adult)

Description

The Citizenship Competencies Program, approved by the Immigration and Naturalization Service (INS), is a self-contained, multi-media curriculum for teaching American history, government, and citizenship, based on the Federal Citizenship Texts and Workbooks. Available at reproduction and handling costs, it is an option for amnesty education, naturalization preparation, and general civics instruction.

The cost for setting up a full program, including instructional materials, computers, software, and video equipment, ranges from $1,400 to $10,000, depending on the equipment ordered.

The ingredients of the program include:

1. The Citizenship Competencies Program breaks down the three Federal Citizenship texts into four levels: (a) U.S. History to the Civil War; (b) U.S. History from the Civil War; (c) Governing Our Nation; and (d) Citizenship Education.

2. These "levels," composed of smaller "units," are each subdivided into three, bite-sized, competency based "lessons" which can be easily mastered in a single learning session.

3. The Citizenship Competencies Program "Implementation Package" includes 14 Curriculum Binders, a Mastery Test binder (diagnostic and prescriptive mastery tests for each unit and level and a global mastery test), a Lesson Assignment Binder with Apple IIe software, a Product Handbook containing user information and tips, and 200 CCP Plan and Profile forms for tracking individual learner progress.

4. Available multi-media options include: Print Supplements, Audio Cassette Supplements, and Voice-Interactive Courseware Supplements.

Contact Person

Andreas Achilla, Special Projects Team Coordinator
U.S. Basics Investment Corp.
1700 Diagonal Road, Suite 400
Alexandria, VA 22314
703-684-1265

• ———— • ———— •

STUDENT ASSISTANCE PROGRAMS
(Self-Concept, Substance Abuse, Teen Parent/Pregnancy, and Other Health-Related Programs)

TITLE OF PROGRAM/Student Assistance
New Holstein/Kiel/Consortium Developed Student Assistance
Program for Neighboring School Districts (Wisconsin)

Level (Elementary, Middle School, and High School)

Description

The New Holstein School District established a need for intervention regarding the problems of alcohol and other drug abuse by students, or problems directly related to drug and alcohol abuse by a family member. Goals were developed to decrease alcohol-related problems in the school, to increase the knowledge of those students referred to the Student Assistance Program regarding alcohol and drugs, and to increase community awareness of the program.

The New Holstein Student Assistance Program is responsible for the identification and referral of students involved, providing resources by which the students can become more knowledgeable, and facilitating appropriate intervention.

The New Holstein Student Assistance Program has benefited the students by developing a core group of faculty, staff, parents, and community members who received, as a result of the program, intensive alcohol and other drug education, thereby enabling them to provide the leadership to coordinate the program. School contact personnel and educational resources have also been developed or purchased. Student groups (use/abuse, support, and after-care) have been developed to aid the students in dealing with the situation.

Thus far, as a result of the program, there has been a decrease in alcohol- and drug-related problems in school. The students involved have shown a decrease in absenteeism, improvement in grades, and a decrease in school suspensions.

The school district community has become aware of the alcohol/drug situation and the Student Assistance Program within the school. Referrals to the program have come from family members, peers, self, and community agencies or institutions.

As a result of the New Holstein Student Assistance Program, students have become more knowledgeable and better able to cope within an environment affected by alcohol and other drugs.

Contact Person
Joseph Wieser
School Districts of New Holstein
2226 Park Avenue
New Holstein, WI 53061
414-893-4208

●————————●————————●

TITLE OF PROGRAM/Student Assistance
Drug Free School Projects (California)

Level (Elementary, Middle School, and High School)

Description
  Several projects under the umbrella of Drug Free Schools exist in various parts of Oakland Unified School District. The Oakland Parks and Recreation Department runs an after-school program in five targeted areas in the city. The centers work on self-esteem issues through organized activities for students. Conciliation Forums focus on training high school students in conflict resolution. Students then use their skills in assisting with conflicts arising within their schools. Peer counseling is offered in both junior highs and high schools. The Narcotics Education League is focusing on assisting bilingual students in making healthy decisions related to drug use and abuse. Various individual school programs such as IMPACT are established in schools throughout the district.

Contact Person
  Dorothy Wilson
  Oakland Unified School District
  1025 2nd Avenue
  Oakland, CA 94606
  415-836-8139

●————— ● ————— ●

TITLE OF PROGRAM/Student Assistance
Police Liaison Program (Wisconsin)

Level (Elementary, Middle School, and High School)
Students between kindergarten and 12th grade who are violators of the law and/or students who are potential violators

Description
  Police officers serve as liaison parties between the schools and police department to teach, counsel, train, and advise as to the legal penalties for certain activities in noncompliance with the law. Liaisons also investigate violations of the law by students or adults who are with students and adults who violate the law against students.

Contact Person
  Lloyd Gutzman
  Green Bay School District
  200 South Broadway
  P.O. Box 1387
  Green Bay, WI 54305
  414-497-3972

●————— ● ————— ●

TITLE OF PROGRAM/Student Assistance
Youth Assistance Programs of Oakland County (Michigan)

Level (Elementary, Middle School, and High School)
Prevention program designed for children who are predelinquent and range in age from birth up to 17 years of age; prevention efforts are also geared towards neglectful situations of children

Description
There is a local Youth Assistance Program in each school district in Oakland County. Caseworkers are assigned to each program to provide counseling services to the clients/families that are referred to them. They also work with volunteers in that particular program, developing and implementing prevention programs that will assist families in broadening their skills as parents which will lead to a reduction in delinquent and neglectful behavior.

Counseling services are voluntary; the client is not a ward of the juvenile court and does not have a court record. Referrals come from parents, school, police, businesses, clergy, etc.; contact is made with the family 48 hours after receiving a referral. If clients require long-term services, the caseworker makes arrangements to refer them to an appropriate agency within the community which will provide the needed services to the family.

Some of the primary prevention programs put on by the local Youth Assistance Programs are camping, youth involvement, youth employment, PLUS (matching a child with a caring adult), Family Education Workshops, recreational activities.

The program is going into its 37th year of existence and approximately 1,200 volunteers are involved. Each local program has a tri-sponsored basis: Probate Court-Juvenile Division, school district, and the municipalities contained within that particular school district.

Contact Person
Mr. Robert Cross, Chief
Oakland County Youth Assistance
1200 North Telegraph Road
Pontiac, MI 48053
313-858-0050

● ———————— ● ———————— ●

TITLE OF PROGRAM/Student Assistance
Alcohol and Drug Abuse Prevention Program (Florida)

Level (Elementary, Middle School, and High School)

Description
Broward County's Alcohol and Drug Abuse Prevention Program uses three components to serve students from kindergarten through high school. Because of its success and cost effectiveness, the program has

been recommended by the Florida Department of Education to serve as a model in Florida's schools. The three components of the program are Information, Process, and Family/Community Service. The information component establishes a drug and alcohol education curriculum in Broward County schools. Techniques in building self-esteem as a weapon against substance abuse are also included. The Process component provides peer counselors as the basis for helping troubled students. Natural leaders are selected from the school population and trained for a full academic year by professionals and receive academic credit. This component also involves a 12-week parenting course for the parents or guardians of problem students. Finally, the Family Counseling/Community Service component provides family counseling services to at-risk families in a nonstigmatic setting at no cost. In addition, there are three substance abuse counselors on the district level who provide intervention, counseling, and case management services for students who are in violation of school substance abuse policy and their parents.

Contact Person

Robert Holsaple, Supervisor of Prevention
   Programs
Broward County Schools
Model Adjustment Program
6650 Griffin Road
Davie, FL 33314
305-765-6537

• ——— • ——— •

TITLE OF PROGRAM/Student Assistance
Transition Program (Oregon)

Level   (Elementary, Middle School, and High School)

Description

Four regions have continued the transition program to improve communication between schools. Teachers of eighth and ninth grade get together to get to know each other and counselors from both schools. Elementary, middle, and middle-high school teachers trade jobs for a few days (fifth/sixth, eighth/ninth); then elementary and middle school students spend a day at the high school in a mock schedule.Those at-risk students meet with counselors in high school during that day. Outcome: Sheldon High School grew larger in enrollment the first year, which was unanticipated. The district has open enrollment and Sheldon usually loses students. There is no evidence that the transition program caused this, but it may have contributed. In late August, prior to school beginning, teachers are paid to visit incoming sixth-grade students at their homes with parents.

Purpose:

1. Comfort level.

2. Explain any information necessary.

3. Let teachers understand the lifestyle conditions of home.

Contact Person
Bob Stalick
Eugene Public Schools
200 North Monroe
Eugene, OR 97402
503-687-3123

● ——— ● ——— ●

TITLE OF PROGRAM/Student Assistance
Police Athletic League (California)

Level (Middle School)

Description
The Oakland Police Department and the Oakland Unified Schools have established a cooperative program at Madison Middle School aimed at designing activities for students after school, weekends, and summers as a means of engaging students. Police personnel volunteer their time in designing and running activities such as weightlifting, basketball, and special interest groups after school and on weekends. The officers run a camp for students in the summer.

Contact Person
Sam Holton
Oakland Police Department
P.O. Box 24376
Oakland, CA 94623
415-568-7333

● ——— ● ——— ●

TITLE OF PROGRAM/Student Assistance
Impact (Colorado)

Level (Middle School and High School)

Description
The Impact program includes prevention and intervention components, suicide crisis team, Students Offering Support (S.O.S.) groups, peer counseling, Youth Excited About Helping (Y.E.A.H.), and a core team of trained faculty members.
The objectives of the Impact program are:

1. To heighten the awareness about chemical dependency, suicide intervention, and family problems, the impact on the school setting, and the role of the school personnel.

2. To offer practical skills for the school professional in the identification, intervention, and referral of chemically dependent students, students who are depressed or suicidal, and students who are not experiencing success in the educational setting.

3. To propose effective school programming and successful implementation of the above-mentioned concepts.

A student referral form is completed and submitted to the Impact Counselor. A member of the Impact Team is assigned (becoming Core Team leader) and contacts all of the student's teachers to see what behaviors are being exhibited. Depending on the behaviors related and the information gathered, a variety of options will be considered. These options include student contract, parent contact, counselor referral, S.O.S. referral, or assessment referral with parental permission to a treatment program. The Core Team leader keeps in contact with the referring person and submits a final report to all involved.

Contact Person
Donna Stefanic, Counselor
Hinkley High School
1250 Chambers Road
Aurora, CO 80011
303-340-1500

● ———— ● ———— ●

TITLE OF PROGRAM/Student Assistance
Alachua County Continuing Education for Pregnant Teens
(ACCEPT) (Florida)

Level   (Middle School and High School)

Description
ACCEPT provides an alternative education program and other services for pregnant teenagers who want to complete middle or high school and learn appropriate skills to enable them to raise a child responsibly. The program's educational objectives include:

1.   The provision of an education program that corresponds to Alachua County standard curriculum so that the student may return to her home school upon program completion.

2.   The offering of individualized instruction to conform to diverse ability and grade levels.

3.   The provision of specialized curriculum in parenting, health, reproduction, sexuality, child health, nutrition, and LaMaze.

The life skills management component includes self-esteem building, career goal setting, life planning, coping skills, and substance abuse prevention. Additional services include day care for infants while parents attend school and work, weekly clinic services provided by the North Central Florida Women's Clinic, a breakfast/lunch program, and bus transportation throughout Alachua County. The onsite infant care allows for an experiential component in child development and parenting skills. The ACCEPT program was established by the School Board of Alachua County in 1979, and is located in the W. Travis Loften Educational Center.

Contact Person
Dr. Ellen West, Principal
The Loften Center
ACCEPT
3000 East University Avenue
Gainesville, FL 32601
904-336-3728
904-336-2842

•————————•————————•

TITLE OF PROGRAM/Student Assistance
Teenage Parent Center Program (Missouri)

Level (Middle School and High School)
School-age parents

Description
The Teenage Parent Center Program was begun in 1971 and has several purposes: to prevent pregnant girls from dropping out of school, to improve the students' educational and job skills, to help maintain and/or improve the health and welfare of the students during pregnancy, childbirth, and the postpartum time of their lives.

The center is staffed by certified personnel, including a nurse, a counselor, and a part-time social worker. The nurse counsels the student about sex, motherhood, the birth process, family relationships, and child care. She acts as a liaison between the school and various health agencies, which are involved in the health care of the student. The responsibilities of the counselor are about the same as those in other secondary schools, including providing career, vocational, and college information. The social worker helps link the student with supportive community services.

The academic program of the Center consists of all levels of English and mathematics, biology, human sciences, civics, world history, current affairs, art and home economics, including family living. Instruction is mostly on an individualized basis. Community resource persons and agencies are used to enrich the program.

As part of the program, the Infant Care Unit was opened in March 1981. It serves as a practicum for students attending the Center. The purpose of the unit is to help develop parenting skills and at the same time provide infant care so that the mothers will be able to continue their education.

Contact Person
Dr. Jasper Harris, Director
Division of Special Education and Pupil
    Services
Kansas City School District
1211 McGee Street
Kansas City, MO 64106
816-221-7565

•————————•————————•

TITLE OF PROGRAM/Student Assistance
Experiential Learning Program (ELP) (Wisconsin)

Level (Middle School and High School)
Potential dropouts, abused children, drug and alcohol abusers, non-goal-directed youth, students with behavior or attitude problems or concerns

Description
This program receives approximately $65,000 from the Department of Public Instruction/Job Training Partnership Act with the Superior School System providing an additional salary for one half-time coordinator for the program. Very generally, the program's purpose is to help meet the education and training needs of economically disadvantaged and at-risk youth. It is designed to help these students in preparing for a general education diploma, provide students with pre-employment and work maturity skills, career assessment, and group counseling in the areas of self-awareness, communication, and decisionmaking skills development, provide one-on-one tutoring for those children in need of special help, work with the Douglas County Chemical Dependency Services within the school system, and help students develop the knowledge, skills, and attitudes necessary for successful employment after graduation or completion of the program.

The program has two components, a seminar class and the work experience. Students receive academic credit for both classes. Both classes are interrelated. The seminar curriculum reinforces and clarifies the work experience element. The classroom instructor serves as the school-work coordinator and works closely with the worksite supervisor and other teachers regarding the child's progress. All students begin as volunteers with the possibility of paid employment upon successful completion of the program's requirements. All program rules and goals are specifically designed to help the child in his or her individual development.

Students are referred to the program by school counselors, administrators, psychologists, chemical dependency staff, or concerned parents. Often community services will refer a student in need.

Goals: Reduce the number of early leavers and dismissals from school, provide general occupational information for students to consider, aid the child in increasing his or her ability to perform academically, motivate the child to understand the world of work and its place in society, help in the development of individual positive attitudes, self-confidence, and relationship-building skills which will help in family, social, and work communication, and help the student receive remedial services when necessary.

Contact Person
Steven Olson, ELP Coordinator
Superior Senior High School
2600 Cotton Avenue
Superior, WI 54880
715-394-0444

TITLE OF PROGRAM/Student Assistance
TLC (Teens Learning to Care): School-Age Parent Program (Michigan)

Level (High School)
An alternative high school completion program serving the needs of young parents and expectant parents and their children

Description
High-school-age students who have children or are pregnant may enroll in TLC. Classes meet Monday through Friday, which allows students to earn up to two and one-half credits per semester. Traditional academic classes are supplemented by instruction on pregnancy, child development, parenting, consumer skills, decisionmaking, and career planning. Group and individual counseling is given by the adult education counselor and a social worker from Family and Children's Services. Oakland County Public Health nurses meet with students each week for health instruction and medical evaluations.

Child care is provided in the nursery and toddler center (state licensed). Families and young fathers may participate in the counseling and support group to assist them in working through problems. TLC provides a supportive atmosphere for the young parent and child.

Contact Person
Karen Eckert, Program Coordinator
Oxford Community Education
105 Pontiac Street
Oxford, MI 48051
313-628-9920

●——— ● ——— ●

TITLE OF PROGRAM/Student Assistance
Tough Love (Michigan)

Level (High School)
Parents of children with behavior, drug, drinking, etc., problems

Description
This is a self-help program using the principles published by David and Phyllis York in their book *Toughlove Solutions* (Bantam Press, 1985). Local groups are already in existence throughout the greater Detroit area, and the country, and the world.

Each group meets weekly; using the guidelines provided in the York book, parents work with each other to achieve changes in their behavior. One of the basic principles is setting a "bottom line"—a limit to behaviors beyond which they become unacceptable—and a consequence for when this "bottom line" is breached. Children learn to be responsible for their actions and learn to take the consequences of their unacceptable behavior. Tough Love groups also work through community resource groups and agencies to find help for their children.

Contact Person
Farmington Group
Maria Schneider
28301 Syke Drive, S
Farmington Hills, MI 48018
313-489-3455

● ——— ● ——— ●

TITLE OF PROGRAM/Student Assistance
Teenage Parent Program (TAP) (Florida)

Level (High School)

Description
Objectives for the program are to continue quality instruction during pregnancy, provide for outreach in the community, and obtain total intake on each student in the program. Other objectives are to help each girl make use of community resources, to counsel students to reduce the possibility of a future unplanned pregnancy, and to develop practical and interpersonal skills for day-to-day living. Other objectives include the transportation of students to and from school and the provision of day care for infants while mothers are in school or working.

Courses offered at TAP are geared to meet the educational needs of the pregnant adolescent. Consideration is given to each student's academic abilities and achievements, with an individual educational plan developed for each student. Home economics, mathematics, typing, recordkeeping, social studies, health, language arts, biology, adaptive physical education, functional skills mathematics, and communications are offered. There is also one class in reading improvement. Infant care, growth and development, and labor and delivery are a part of the health/biology curriculum taught by the TAP nurse. Adaptive physical education includes pre- and postnatal exercises with emphasis on breathing exercises to be used during delivery (LaMaze method). Girls taking courses not offered at TAP are instructed on an individual basis.

Support curriculum consists of classes in infant stimulation offered through the TAP-4-C Nursery and enrichment activities. Social services offered are: small-group counseling; individual counseling when needed; home visits; and referrals to other agencies. Breakfast and lunch are served to students in a cafeteria shared with the School for Applied Individualized Learning (SAIL). Nutritional snacks are sold in the morning in order to encourage good nutrition.

TAP is currently funded through alternative education. Other funding comes from vocational education. TAP day care is provided by Leon County 4-Council through a cooperative agreement with the school system, using Title XX monies. The nursing position at TAP is funded under Title V and coordinated through HRS and the Leon County Health Department.

Contact Person
   Seaton K. Bradford
   Program Manager, TAP
   438 West Brevard Street
   Tallahassee, FL 32304
   904-488-5400

● ———— ● ———— ●

TITLE OF PROGRAM/Student Assistance
   OMBUDSMAN (North Carolina)

Level   (High School)

Description
   OMBUDSMAN is a structured course designed to reduce certain psychological and attitudinal states closely related to drug use. OMBUDSMAN does not emphasize information about drugs per se, although some drug topics are included for discussion as part of specific exercises.
   The course has three major phases. The first phase focuses on self-awareness and includes a series of exercises permitting students to gain a wider understanding and appreciation of their values as autonomous individuals. The second phase teaches group skills and provides students with an opportunity to develop communication, decisionmaking, and problem-solving techniques that can be applied in the immediate class situation as well as in other important group contexts such as with family and peers. The third phase is in many ways the most important. The class uses the insights and skills gained during the first two phases to plan and carry out a project within the community or school. During this phase, students have an opportunity to experience the excitement and satisfaction of reaching out to others in a creative and constructive way. The program must be presented to a given classroom of students for a minimum of two hours per week for a full semester.

Contact Person
   Jay Keny, Dissemination Coordinator
   Charlotte Drug Education Center
   1416 East Morehead
   Charlotte, NC 28204
   704-336-3211

● ———— ● ———— ●

TITLE OF PROGRAM/Student Assistance
   HOLD: Helping Overcome Learner Dropouts: 9 through 12
   (California)

Level   (High School)

Description
   A prescriptive counseling program designed to maintain enrollment of potential dropouts by increasing attendance, self-esteem, and academic success through peer counseling, attendance monitoring, parent counseling, and classroom guidance. The program was disseminated during the Sharing Educational Success Traveling Seminars in 1982.

Contact Person
Joan Rost
Pajaro Valley Unified School District
550 Rodrigues Street
Watsonville, CA 95076
408-728-6330

● ———— ● ———— ●

TITLE OF PROGRAM/Student Assistance
Family Life Education Center (FLEC) (Michigan)

Level (High School)
Any teenage pregnant girl in the school district who wishes to continue her education during the course of her pregnancy

Description
Program objectives:

1. To provide pregnant teens with an accredited school program to continue toward graduation.

2. To provide the special needs of proper prenatal and postnatal care, child care, and child development including the LaMaze classes.

3. To provide remedial and individualized instruction in academics, health and home, and family living.

Referrals: Students may be referred by counselor or principal and may return to regular classes at any suitable semester break.

Contact Person
William D. Kimball, Assistant Superintendent
2720 Riverside Drive
Port Huron, MI 48060
313-885-3510

● ———— ● ———— ●

TITLE OF PROGRAM/Student Assistance
Peer Counseling (Colorado)

Level (High School)

Description
The purpose of peer counseling (peer facilitating) is for all students to have the opportunity to discuss personal concerns with a trained peer. In addition, new students receive a personal orientation and welcome to the school. Students selected to serve as peer counselors are trained to form one-to-one helping relationships, to provide group discussion leadership, to provide pertinent information, and to make appropriate referrals. Peer Counselors are supervised by the professional counseling staff.
Unique Features:

1. Peer Counselors are trained for nine weeks in a class that meets daily.

2. Peer Counselors act as liaisons for students with adult helpers in the building.

3. Peer Counselors learn about community resources.

4. Peer Counselors work with middle school students to help with transition activities.

5. Peer Counselors act as resources and helpers for teachers and programs within their respective schools.

Contact Person
Jeanie Johnson, Counselor
Gateway High School
1300 South Sable Boulevard
Aurora, CO 80012
303-755-7160

• ———— • ———— •

TITLE OF PROGRAM/Student Assistance
S.O.S. Groups (Students Offering Support) (Colorado)

Level   (High School)

Description
        S.O.S. groups are a major in-school component of the Impact program. Support groups are "growth-centered": students learn to cope more effectively with their daily developmental concerns and remediate personal conflicts. The task of the counselor is to facilitate the group process and help students achieve greater self-awareness, self-understanding, and self-responsibility and to help them to recognize, appreciate, respect, value, and support other persons in their lives. Counseling groups can provide the fundamental conditions necessary for students to help each other and to receive the good feelings associated with the helping process. Group members learn rules for getting along, cooperating, and respecting others' ways that will enhance their personal growth and development. It is also one of the most effective ways to break into the systems of cliques. When groups are organized, students from different social groups are deliberately placed into a single counseling group.
        In "growth-centered" groups, students are encouraged to discuss their thoughts, feelings, and behaviors, and to compare themselves with their peers. As students learn to get support, identify problems, express feelings, and make rational decisions, they often find they are able to make better choices and often begin to demonstrate better attitudes toward school. Direct involvement in groups allows students invaluable opportunities to increase their planning, goal setting, decisionmaking, organizing, and communication skills. Groups operate as learning laboratories in which students gain self-acceptance, social skills, inner strength, and self-discipline. Students learn that with the help of friends, they can begin to deal with problems that previously discouraged or even defeated them. They learn and model for their peers assertiveness, problem solving, coping skills, and more effective communication skills.
        During the hours they spend in groups, students often wrestle with major emotional issues. They find that counseling is hard work. The group experience is a powerful tool for helping adolescent students make

positive changes in their lives, changes they may not be readily able to make on their own or in their own peer groups. It is the counselor's responsibility to foster the therapeutic conditions of confidentiality, trust, acceptance, support, and cohesiveness.

Students are placed in S.O.S. groups mostly by self-referral, but peer, parents, staff, and counselor referrals are also accepted. Students are interviewed by a counselor prior to placement in groups. Group composition reflects the diversity of the student body. S.O.S. groups are open to all students.

Contact Person
Donna Stefanic, Counselor
Hinkley High School
1250 Chambers Road
Aurora, CO 80011
303-340-1500

●————— ● ————— ●

TITLE OF PROGRAM/Student Assistance
GATEWAY ALIVE (Colorado)

Level (High School)

Description
GATEWAY ALIVE is a group of students against drug and alcohol abuse. They believe that education about substance abuse and prevention strategies is the best means to help students say "no" to drugs and alcohol.

Students are chosen to be members of GATEWAY ALIVE through personal interest, teacher recommendations, and a personal interview.

In 1988, members of GATEWAY ALIVE visited Aurora Hills Middle School to discuss substance abuse with some classes. They sponsored an "Awareness Day" and distributed pencils imprinted with "Gateway Alive says 'No' to Drugs & Alcohol."

Through speakers, films, group discussion, and various workshop activities, students learn about themselves and how to better relate to others. They learn not only how to say "no" to drugs and alcohol, but also how to demonstrate refusal skills. Drug and alcohol prevention is stressed, along with decisionmaking skills, assertiveness training, dealing with stress and grief, and improving self-image.

Contact Person
Marcia Krett, Counselor
Gateway High School
1300 South Sable Boulevard
Aurora, CO 80012
303-755-7160

●————— ● ————— ●

VOCATIONAL AND WORK/STUDY PROGRAMS

TITLE OF PROGRAM/Vocational, Work/Study
Work Experience Career Exploration Program (WECEP)
(Wisconsin)

Level (Middle School
Potential dropouts

Description
This program is designed to provide support in educational, vocational, and career awareness opportunities for potential school dropouts at the junior high school level. Students who are 14 and 15 years old, are academically or economically disadvantaged, and who show one or more dysfunctional behaviors or attitudes that act as barriers to successful participation at school may participate. Key criteria for participation are an inability to function properly within a regular classroom setting, a record of absenteeism and tardiness, lack of motivation and direction, behavior problems, repeated suspension and referrals to the office for discipline, and failure to establish meaningful goals for the future. WECEP provides relevant classroom experience opportunities for these at-risk students. It combines regular course work, an employability skills class, and an opportunity to have a regular paying job in the community. School credit is awarded for successful performance on the job and in the related classes.

Contact Person
Carolyn Hughes
Neenah School District
410 South Commercial Street
Neenah, WI 54956
414-729-6850

● ———— ● ———— ●

TITLE OF PROGRAM/Vocational, Work/Study
Winter Park Compact, Winter Park High School (Florida)

Level (High School)

Description
In an endeavor to solve dropout problems and prevent potential dropouts from leaving school, Winter Park High School developed a dropout reduction program, modeling it after the Boston Compact. In the Boston Compact, agreements were created between Boston public high schools and the business community in which businesses would give graduates hiring priority if schools improved their graduates' educational achievement. The three major goals of the program are: (1) to develop a system to identify potential dropouts before a decision to drop out has been made; (2) to provide help and counseling for potential dropouts from social service personnel and an occupational specialist. The occupational specialist makes a compact with the student whereby the student

will remain in school, improve attendance and grades, and be rewarded by being hired by local businesses; (3) to retrieve dropouts back into school with the incentive of a job offer. The program also features involvement with parents of potential dropouts, small classes, and assignment to special teachers who have an interest in working with potential dropouts. Courses in occupational skills and field trips to businesses are also offered.

A student assistance program component has been added to help students with many problems.

Contact Person
Bruce L. Suther, Assistant Principal
Winter Park High School
2100 Summerfield Road
Orlando, FL 32792
305-644-6921

● —————— ● —————— ●

TITLE OF PROGRAM/Vocational, Work/Study
Project COFFEE (Cooperative Federation for Educational Experiences) (Florida)

Level   (High School)

Description
Project COFFEE is a regional dropout prevention/reclamation program which targets 120 at-risk secondary school students from 18 school districts whose academic history includes grade retention, truancy, high absenteeism, and disruptive behavior. The curricular components include basic skills, occupational education, group and individual counseling, pre-employment education, daily living skills, experimental learning, and computer-assisted instruction.

Each occupational program features job entry skills, job placement skills, shadowing experiences, and a related work-study program. Occupational components include: Computer Maintenance/Repair, Word Processing, Building and Grounds Maintenance, Horticulture/Agriculture, and Distributive Education. Project COFFEE was developed by a regional cooperative federation of seven school districts and a highly successful partnership with high technology business and industry. This partnership has provided educational assistance in curriculum development, staff training, occupational training materials, equipment acquisition, competency based assessments, internship experiences, and more. Materials include: program manual, basic skills curriculum guide, guidelines for industry/education linkage, guidelines for interagency collaboration/community outreach, procedures manual for development of competency based assessments, and a diagnostic needs assessment survey manual for a student survival skills course. The program functions as a school within a school.

Contact Person
Sean M. Gilrein, Project Director
Michael Fields, COFFEE NDN Coordinator
Project COFFEE
Oxford High School Annex
Main Street
Oxford, MA 01540
617-987-2591

● ———— ● ———— ●

TITLE OF PROGRAM/Vocational, Work/Study
Operation Success (New York)

Level   (High School)

Description
Provide support services to high school students, both dropouts and those at risk of dropping out. Services include Case Management, Diagnostic Vocational Evaluation, Vocational Skills Training, Educational Internships (work experience), Career and Vocational Exploration, personal and family counseling and referrals, and part-time job development and employment.

Subsequent to the establishment of Operation Success, initially funded by the New York State Education Department, and operated within the public schools in cooperation with the New York City Board of Education and the United Federation of Teachers, Operation Success was recognized in the Federal Register of 1985 as a model program, was the forerunner in dropout prevention programs across the country, and was cited as a model for New York State in its establishment of the State's Attendance Improvement Dropout Prevention (AIDP) funds.

Contact Person
Rae Linefsky, Senior Vice President
Federation Employment & Guidance Service
62 West 14th Street, 7th Floor
New York, NY 10011
212-741-7581

● ———— ● ———— ●

TITLE OF PROGRAM/Vocational, Work/Study
Total Career Assessment Program (California)

Level   (High School)

Description
The Total Career Assessment Program is a systematic and sequential approach to career education for high school students grades 9 to 12. The program is specifically developed to meet the identified career education needs of rural youth, but is suitable for the general secondary population as well as students in continuation high schools. The materials and

activities are designed to be infused into the academic curriculum as a means of reinforcing the basic skills and teaching key career education concepts.

Career education is a lifelong process that begins in the early years. The Total Career Assessment Program provides secondary students with self-assessment, decisionmaking strategies, job search skills, career option exploration, and an individual career plan. A team approach including parents, teachers, counselors, administrators, and community members furnishes total carrythrough of key concepts at each grade level. Since career education is not a separate subject, concepts and lessons should be infused into all subject areas.

Contact Person
Craig Allen
Humboldt County Office of Education
Project T.E.E.M.
2501 Cypress Avenue
Eureka, CA 95501
707-445-7068

• —————— • —————— •

TITLE OF PROGRAM/Vocational, Work/Study
Summer Youth Employment & Training Program (SYETP),
J.T.P.A. (Missouri)

Level   (High School)
Economically disadvantaged 14- to 15-year-old students who are potential dropouts because of poor attendance, low achievement, etc., who must qualify under J.T.P.A. guidelines

Description
The SYETP is a six-week summer program whose purpose is to provide career education and exploration to 14- to 15-year-old potential dropouts so that when they become 16 years of age they decide to remain in school to obtain their high school diploma. In 1989, the 9th year of the program, 114 students from 10 school districts in St. Louis County participated.

The program is structured so that students attend four hours per day at their home school with a teacher. Because it is a training program, the students spend about 50 percent of that time in a classroom situation where they learn information related to preparing for employment (e.g., completing job application, interest survey, etc.). The remaining 50 percent of the time is spent on field trips to companies and training schools throughout the St. Louis area where students hear directly from employers what they look for in employees. They also get to tour these companies and see many jobs first hand.

Students do not earn pay but do receive a $10.00 daily stipend for transportation and lunch expenses. In addition, upon successful completion of the program they earn 1/2 unit of high school credit. Follow-up studies show that more than 90 percent of the participants remain enrolled in school after reaching age 16, and more than 80 percent eventually graduate. Their attendance, grades, and citizenship improve as compared to the year prior to entering the program.

Contact Person
W. D. Leip, Director
J.T.P.A. Programs
Ritenour School District
3238 Marshall Avenue
St. John, MO 63114
314-429-1088

● —————— ● —————— ●

TITLE OF PROGRAM/Vocational, Work/Study
Summer Youth Employment Training Program (California)

Level   (High School)

Description
The students' jobs are to be tutors, but as tutors the tutors themselves learn. There was a remarkable test score improvement of tutors.

About 90 Oakland school children are being paid minimum wage to work both as students and teachers as part of a new summer youth employment program that supporters say may be the only one of its kind. The six-week project is administered jointly by the Oakland Unified School District and the city and paid for with federal job-training funds.

It is designed to help students master basic academic skills and to teach them to pass their knowledge along to other public school students with special needs. The program targets economically disadvantaged students whose academic skills lag two or three years below their grade level.

Tutors in the new program spent their first three weeks boning up on basic English and math skills and the next three weeks teaching.

Contact Person
Cecilia Bennett
Oakland Unified School District
1025 2nd Avenue, Portable 15
Oakland, CA 94606
415-836-8139

● —————— ● —————— ●

TITLE OF PROGRAM/Vocational, Work/Study
Vocational Village Program (Oregon)

Level   (High School)

Description
A former factory building in southeast Portland offers the benefits of a small school setting for Vocational Village. The small size offers individualized attention and gives the students a sense of ownership. Students take pride in the building and the care of it.

The enrollment in this complete high school is around 200 during the day and 65 in the evening classes. The program serves students who have dropped out of traditional high schools, ages 12 to 21, and is especially designed for students who have academic, economic, physical, or emotional problems.

The academic program at the school is self-paced and performance-based. Motivated students are able to earn credits faster than at a regular high school. Each student is a vocational student. Two hours are spent each day in the vocational cluster of the student's choice.

The school offers classes in child care, food service, graphics, industrial mechanics, marketing, office practice, metals and welding, health occupations, and electronics.

Contact Person
Alcena Boozer, Alternative Education
    Supervisor
Portland Public Schools
P.O. Box 3107
Portland, OR 97208
503-280-5783

FAMILY SUPPORT PROGRAMS
(Parent Programs)

TITLE OF PROGRAM/Family Support
Parent Place (Wisconsin)

Level (Elementary)
Parents of children at risk

Description
This is a family support and training program for children in the Stoughton Area School District. The main focus is on parents of Chapter I students and parents of preschool- through high-school-age children who have been identified as being from families with characteristics which negatively influence a child's success in the school and community.

The overall goal of Parent Place is to provide a unique approach to parent involvement, knowing that any kind of well-planned, comprehensive, and long-lasting parent involvement tends to improve school performance of students.

The major objective of Parent Place is to increase student academic achievement. The secondary objective of Parent Place is to increase parent knowledge about effective parenting strategies, including behavior management techniques and the importance of parental modeling. The Stoughton Area School District believes that to be the most effective in assuring a student's success in school, a student must be worked with in the context of his or her total environment — community, family, and school.

Contact Person
Ellen Leggett, Parent Place Coordinator
Stoughton Area School District
211 North Forest Street
Stoughton, WI 53589-0189
608-873-7257

● —————— ● —————— ●

TITLE OF PROGRAM/Family Support
Elementary Home-School Liaison (Colorado)

Level (Elementary)

Description
Under the direction of the building administration and within the parameters of District goals and objectives, the home-school liaison demonstrates knowledge and appropriate strategies for dealing with the pre-adolescent student, identifies alternatives for students, and assists parents and staff in developing a positive educational environment. The home-school liaison serves as an intermediary between the school and

home, making parental contacts and home visits dealing with chronic academic, behavioral, attendance, and truancy problems. Responsibilities include:

1. Carrying out intervention strategies to obtain increased attendance and punctuality on the part of students whose nonattendance or tardiness is unexcused or suspected of being so.

   a. Conducting personal conferences with students and parents regarding absence, tardiness, and academic and social progress.

   b. Providing instructional assistance in certain situations in order to facilitate student skill acquisition for the time absent.

2. Assisting parents in the home setting to provide motivation to improve student attendance and punctuality as well as academic performance.

   a. Coordinating community resources which may be needed by the student/parent in order to maintain student attendance and punctuality.

3. Developing an ongoing orientation plan for mobile students and conducting the sessions on a recurring basis.

4. Serving as a resource to school staff in dealing with special student needs not covered by special education services.

5. Serving as a resource in child abuse cases, special education staffing, and contacts with other community/governmental agencies.

Contact Person
Vince Dattolo
Aurora Public Schools
1085 Peoria
Aurora, CO 80011
303-344-8060

●————— ● ————— ●

TITLE OF PROGRAM/Family Support
Suicide Prevention Training Manual (Pennsylvania)

Level (Elementary, Middle School, and High School)
Parents and teachers of children at risk

Description
This is a 14-lesson course for adults which will help them deal with the facts about suicide in a manner which leads to understanding of and empathy with the suicidal person. It focuses on improving the individual's ability to recognize a suicidal person and increasing the individual's knowledge of what steps to take to prevent suicide attempts. This is geared to suicide in general and can be used to train a community, much like CPR training. Cost $12.00.

"If Someone You Know Is Thinking about Suicide, You Can Help!" is a single-sheet information piece listing the warning signs of suicide and giving brief tips on how to help prevent suicide. This is geared to be used in a classroom/community education setting to stimulate discussion. Available free of charge.

Contact Person

Merck Sharp and Dohme
North Wales Press, Inc.
P.O. Box 1486
North Wales, PA 19454
215-377-4490

ATTENDANCE/TRUANCY
PREVENTION PROGRAMS

TITLE OF PROGRAM/Attendance/Truancy Prevention
Absentee Prevention Program (APP) (Pennsylvania)

Level (Elementary through Middle School [K to 8])

Description

The Absentee Prevention Program (APP) is designed to identify high-risk, chronically absent, and tardy students in the elementary grades. This involves investigating and determining the causes of absenteeism, and providing appropriate intervention/prevention services for these students, their families, and teachers.

Absenteeism is viewed as a symptom of other problems.

The goal is to reduce the number of absences in the target group and help prevent a pattern of future absenteeism. Services include: home visits, school conferences, phone consultations, collaboration with/and referrals to social service agencies, parenting skills workshops, teacher inservice training, teacher conferences, individual counseling, and personal growth groups.

The APP has a research design and has shown statistically significant results in improving attendance.

The program has been replicated in schools throughout the nation. It is a model for Pennsylvania Department of Health, Michigan Department of Mental Health, and New Jersey Department of Education.

Contact Person

Anna Mae Paladina, Coordinator of Primary
    Prevention
Prevention Project
Community College of Beaver County
College Drive
Monaca, PA 15061
412-775-8561, ext. 159

● ——————— ● ——————— ●

TITLE OF PROGRAM/Attendance/Truancy Prevention
Attendance Incentive — A Reward System for Perfect
Attendance (Pennsylvania)

Level (Elementary, Middle School, and High School)
All grade levels

Description

The following reward system was developed by Northern Potter High School.

1. One semester perfect attendance entitles the student to a free pass to all school events for the following semester. These will be issued by the office and signed by the principal.

2. A full year of perfect attendance exempts the student from final exams for that year.

3. At graduation, students will be presented with a certificate of perfect attendance for each year of perfect attendance.

   In most instances, the success of a program is determined in the implementation stage of the program. This attendance reward system resulted in 78 percent of the student body having perfect attendance — for any reason and with no exceptions. When exceptions are part of a program, then judgments have to be made. It is critical that students perceive the whole notion as fair and attainable. As long as school is in session and providing a full program, students are required to attend. (This answered snow-day questions.) Bussing is part of the program offered by the school: if the bus does not arrive, the student is not held accountable.

   Suggested guidelines are:

1. Make *no* exceptions to the perfect attendance rule, regardless of cause.

2. Consider school-sponsored activities as students being in attendance, i.e., field trips, college visitations, etc.

3. Insist on mid-term examinations so that students still have the *experience* of a final exam.

4. Establish the time at which the morning session is half gone, so that the issue of truancy is not confused with absenteeism. If over half the morning session is not attended, the student is absent half a day.

5. Establish the time at which the afternoon session is half completed. This accommodates early dismissals for appointments, etc., and still has the student in session for the major portion of the afternoon.

   The purpose in issuing student passes to all school affairs following a semester of perfect attendance was to encourage students to work for perfect attendance even though they missed one or two days in the year. They do not need to wait a whole year to try again. This is a goal to work on each semester. Naturally, they are only exempt from final exams for yearly perfect attendance, but free passes to school events is based on *semester* attendance and does not destroy the initiative to try for perfect attendance. We used these guidelines in implementing the free student passes:

1. The same time frame established for late arrivals in the early dismissal session is used in the afternoon session to determine whether a half day was missed.

2. Passes were printed in limited quantities.

3. Unsigned passes are counted and kept in the principal's desk.

4. After attendance, officers identify students with perfect attendance; the principal distributes exact number of passes to secretaries for typing students' names on passes.

5. Passes are not valid until the principal signs the pass. We did not use a signature stamp.

6. "Ticket takers" at school functions are aware of free student pass policy.

The student pass policy applied to school-sponsored affairs held at the home school. This avoided the problem of enlisting the cooperation of others in the case of interscholastic sports.

Contact Person
Shirley D. Ball, Ph.D., Superintendent
Lehighton Area School District
200 Beaver Run Road
Lehighton, PA 18235
215-377-4490

● ———— ● ———— ●

TITLE OF PROGRAM/Attendance/Truancy Prevention
OASIS (California)

Level (Middle School)

Description
Project OASIS (Opportunity at Suspension in Schools) is an alternative to a suspension program for students who are removed from the classroom for misbehavior. The project continues to provide supervision and instruction for students. The entire school climate benefits because all students need a safe, quiet, learning environment free from threats, harassment, and nonproductive noise. When disturbances happen within the classroom, students may be sent to OASIS in lieu of suspension. This reduces the total number of school suspensions and continues the educational process for students. Students need to have alternatives to suspension in an attempt to correct disruptive behavior and return to the school population as soon as possible. Although the program was developed at the junior-high-school level, it is applicable with both elementary grade and high-school level students.

Contact Person
Shereene D. Wilkerson, Assistant Principal
Willis Jepson Junior High School
580 Elder Street
Vacaville, CA 95688
707-446-6829

● ———— ● ———— ●

TITLE OF PROGRAM/Attendance/Truancy Prevention
Lansing School District Re-Entry (Michigan)

Level (Middle School)
Middle school students—Grades six, seven, and eight

Description

Design

1. The program is set up to meet the needs of students who have been unable to succeed in the traditional, middle school for such reasons as: truancy or poor attendance, low achievement, lack of self-discipline, and behavioral problems.

2. The program serves students from the ages of eleven to fourteen. The program mainstreams Special Education students into the regular classes.

Referrals

1. Students can be referred to middle school alternative programs from the following sources: primarily assistant principals and counselors, occasionally caseworkers and probation officers with the Department of Social Services and Probate Court, and also personnel in Student Services.

2. The process of admittance is initiated by Student Services personnel and by the assistant principal or counselor from the sending school. The student will be referred to the middle school alternative site where an interview with the instructor, the parent, and the student will be conducted for admittance.

Instruction

1. Instruction is based upon curriculum requirements established by the Lansing School District for middle school.

2. Curriculum is primarily based on remediation in math and English.

3. Regular attendance is critical to student success in the program.

Contact Person

Thomas McClellan, Administrator
Alternative Education Program
1030 South Holmes Street
Lansing, MI 48912
517-374-4223

●───── ● ───── ●

TITLE OF PROGRAM/Attendance/Truancy Prevention
Positive Alternatives to Student Suspensions (PASS) (Florida)

Level   (Middle School and High School)

Description

PASS is a program that offers several solution strategies for serious behavior problems that often result in student suspensions. Given that a high number of suspensions increase the propensity of a student to drop out of school, Pinellas County developed preventive/developmental and crisis/remedial interventions, responding to the problem in a comprehesive way.

Prevention/developmental activities include:

- Staff development for a humanistic school—Workshops and seminars to help school faculty and staff learn to communicate positively, thus creating a more humane atmosphere
- Humanistic activities in the regular classroom—Psychologists, social workers, and teachers direct a 12-week program in which students spend an hour a week in positive social awareness activities that foster a feeling of belonging
- Basic encounter for school personnel—The faculty/staff version of the student encounter program
- Parent training groups—A six-session program that helps parents improve relationships with their children.

The crisis/remedial components include the following:

- The time-out room—A strategy that provides an alternative learning environment in which students can discuss problems with a "listener" before coping difficulties result in undesirable behavior
- A school survival course—A 12-week program that helps students with behavior problems learn to create positive learning experiences and positive feedback from teachers and other students, thereby decreasing misbehavior and suspensions
- A home survival course—A 12-week program that teaches students a variety of techniques to facilitate relationships at home.

Students participating in PASS programs have experienced a significantly lower frequency of misbehavior and suspensions than previous data have shown. The program is supported by state and local funds.

Major activities of the PASS program include individual and group consultations that assist school faculties in developing techniques for dealing effectively with teenage students, affective education and personal development programs for students and teachers, time-out rooms managed by a teacher or paraprofessional where students talk out problems and complete academic assignments, individual and group counseling for students experiencing serious interpersonal confrontations, and counseling for parents.

"Staff Development for a Positive School" and "Communication Activities in the Regular Classroom" help students and teachers get to know and appreciate each other. "A Student's School Survival Course" and "Home Survival Source" help students with problems and learn how to interact more effectively within their school and home environments.

Contact Person

John C. Kackley, Supervisor/Consultant
or Ralph E. Bailey, Director, Project PASS
Pupil Personnel Services Demonstration Project
Euclid Center
1015 Tenth Avenue North
St. Petersburg, FL 33705
813-823-6696, ext. 45

TITLE OF PROGRAM/Attendance/Truancy Prevention
In-School Suspension Program—Warren Consolidated Schools
(Michigan)

Level   (Middle School and High School)
Junior high school students (Grades 7 to 9);
senior high school students (Grades 10 to 12)

Description

The In-School Suspension Program provides an alternative to out-of-school suspension for students who have violated school policies.

One of the purposes of the program is to provide a more effective form of discipline. Instead of being sent home for a suspension, the student remains in school, but completely isolated from the student body in a structured environment.

The length of the suspension may vary from one to ten days depending on the severity of the offense. During the student's confinement in the suspension room, class assignments and testing continue. The student is required to complete all assigned work and adhere to the strict regulations of the In-School Suspension Program.

Classroom teachers receive notification of the student's suspension and the request for assignments. Completed homework and tests are returned to the classroom teachers who then determine the grades for the completed work.

While in the program the students are expected to improve attitude, to modify behavior, to complete academic work, to strive for academic success, and to cope with life in a socially acceptable manner.

The In-School Suspension Program serves the total secondary population of Warren consolidated schools. The program is housed in two junior high school facilities and in two senior high school facilities.

The student's parents are responsible for transportation to the appropriate In-house Suspension facility.

While in the In-School Suspension Program:

- Students are on a staggered schedule

- They are expected to arrive on time

- They are expected to leave the building and grounds immediately upon dismissal

- No formal lunch period is provided, but the student may bring a sack lunch

- Students are not to talk to anyone except the teacher

- Absences from school do not count as assigned days in the program

- Student misbehavior will result in additional assigned days or exclusion from school.

Upon completion of the In-School Suspension Program, the student returns to his regular class schedule.

Contact Person

Daniel L. Schafer, Alternative Education Specialist
Warren Consolidated Schools
Sterling Heights High School
12901 Fifteen Mile Road
Sterling Heights, MI 48077
313-939-5900, ext. 65

● ———— ● ———— ●

TITLE OF PROGRAM/Attendance/Truancy Prevention
Positive Approach to Good Attendance through Grading (Iowa)

Level (High School)
Designed to encourage students and their parents to understand the importance of attending school regularly

Description

Roll is taken daily first hour by the central office and recorded. All students absent are contacted by 9:15 if school has not been notified by a parent. Roll is also taken each period by the teacher and recorded in the grade book or daily log book. The central office attendance record and each of the seven periods may differ as much as five days during a nine-week grading period. Students arriving late, leaving early, etc., will make this difference.

Grades are figures for each student in each class at the end of the nine weeks. The grading curve is established and each student has a grade based on academic achievement.

Each teacher then looks in his or her grade book or daily log and checks attendance. The following scale is used on attendance.

Perfect attendance in their class - 10 percent bonus

One day absent in their class   - 9 percent bonus

Two days absent in their class   - 8 percent bonus

Three days absent in their class - 7 percent bonus

Four days absent in their class - 6 percent bonus

Five days absent in their class - 5 percent bonus

Six days absent in their class   - 4 percent bonus

Seven days absent in their class - 3 percent bonus

Eight days absent in their class - 2 percent bonus

Nine days absent in their class - 1 percent bonus

The teacher takes these bonus points and adds them to each student's academic points; thus, his or her grade can improve, depending on how many bonus points are added to the individual student. Caution: To assure no grade is lowered, do not add attendance bonus points to academic points until after the grade scale has been established.

A student is not counted absent if he or she is involved in another school activity that has been arranged by the school.

This system can help a student raise a grade from a C +, for example, to a B − and possibly a B, depending on the number of attendance bonus points. The system is especially helpful for a lower-ability student who is in attendance almost daily but really is struggling. This gives some reward for attending regularly and in many cases permits these students to pass the course.

Contact Person
Mr. Robert D. Blasi, Senior High Principal
East 4th Street
Glenwood, IA 51534
712-527-4897

● ———— ● ———— ●

TITLE OF PROGRAM/Attendance/Truancy Prevention
A Positive Alternative to Pupil Suspensions, Truancy, and
Dropout (New York)

Level   (High School)
Approved by JDRP for students in grades 9 through 12 who have high rates of failure and truancy along with a history of disruptive behavior

Description
A teacher-training program that addresses problems of student discipline, truancy, and chronic academic failure.

Project Intercept provides preservice/inservice training about failing and truant behavior, to address such problems before these difficulties fully develop. A preservice/inservice training program offers teachers training in four areas.

All staff in the program are taught effective discipline procedures, classroom management techniques, and instructional skills. A peer consulting team is developed for group critique and support.

Management skills for establishing an alternative academic program for potential dropouts are also taught. Three programs developed by Project Intercept are COPE, Learning Center, and the Learning Cluster. In the first two programs, targeted satudents are placed in self-contained classes for two-thirds of the day, and may take electives or attend vocational training programs during the remainder of the day. The Learning Cluster offers a preventive treatment program to ninth grade students where one-quarter of the day is spent in English and social studies.

Teachers also receive training in group counseling; students who participate in this component learn to demonstrate more appropriate interpersonal skills and improved self-concept. Family intervention and parent training skills are taught to staff who are responsible for parent contact. This component reinforces changes taking place at school and helps parents deal more effectively with all their children.

Contact Person
Richard Maurer, Ph.D.
Anne M. Dornor Middle School
Van Cortlandt Avenue
Ossining, NY 10562
914-762-5740

● ———— ● ———— ●

TITLE OF PROGRAM/Attendance/Truancy Prevention
Alternative to Suspension (California)

Level   (High School)

Description
      Students who are faced with suspension from school are given the alternative to work at maintenance jobs at the school on Saturday morning (washing windows, sweeping, and cleaning). The group varies from one to six students, and informal counseling during the morning gives students a break from work. While in the program, students are placed in a separate classroom and are exposed to independent study techniques to improve their education. This program has been in operation since 1978, when it was designated a Noteworthy Practice by the State Department of Education.

Contact Person
      Shereen D. Wilkerson
      Willis Jepson Junior High
      580 Elder Street
      Vacaville, CA 85688
      707-446-6829

●———— ● ———— ●

TITLE OF PROGRAM/Attendance/Truancy Prevention
Positive Discipline Program (Maryland)

Level   (High School)

Description
      The goals of the project are fourfold. They are to create a more positive image of the school in the community, recognize appropriate student behavior, place the individual instructor in a positive position with respect to his or her students and those students' families, and reinforce contributions of the staff members to the school.
      This program uses a number of positive public relations techniques which have been most effective in promoting higher school attendance on the part of the students.
      In dealing with individual students, we find the student engaged in some positive activity and recognize him or her for it. Some of the recognition has come from good attendance.
      Annually, this county enjoys the highest or second best attendance in the state of Maryland.

Contact Person
      James H. VanSciver, Principal
      Pocomoke High School
      R.F.D. 2
      Box 195
      Pocomoke City, MD 21851
      301-957-1484

●———— ● ———— ●

BUSINESS- AND
COMMUNITY-RELATED PROGRAMS

TITLE OF PROGRAM/Business- and Community-Related
　Scholar/Athlete Program (Georgia)

Level　(High School)

Description

　　Scholar/Athlete Program is an adopt-a-student program dealing with at-risk students and dropouts and matching them with business and industry member for one-to-one for a couple of years.

　　Mentor — Big Brother/Big Sister program, middle and high school — two years — The Atlanta Public Schools Mentor Program. Through a joint venture with the Atlanta Exchange, Big Brothers/Big Sisters of Metropolitan Atlanta (BB/BS) and the Atlanta Public Schools, the Mentor Program is becoming a reality for approximately 250 students.

　　To assist with implementation of this program, computer systems have been placed in counselors' offices in all secondary and middle schools in Atlanta. These computers provide both counselors and students with access to a mainframe computer at Georgia State University with data on 260 occupations, colleges and universities throughout the nation, and numerous financial aid programs.

　　Goals of the Mentor Program:

1.　One-to-one career counseling.

2.　Direct access to businesses and professional persons.

3.　Expand and enhance the career counseling capability of Metro Atlanta Public schools.

4.　Involve businesses and professional persons directly in the career development.

5.　Encourage students to become successful business persons and professionals.

　　The program officially began in October 1986, with orientation sessions provided for coaches, counselors, sports captains, and student participants. The format of the program includes a 30-minute enrichment session each morning prior to the beginning of the school day. On Mondays, Wednesdays, and Fridays of each week, the potential athletes will receive tutorial services from college students, teachers, and/or peers. The tutorial sessions will be individualized, based on a needs assessment and teacher input. The teachers of the program participants will be requested to indicate the area of study for his or her subject to be targeted in tutorial sessions. The purpose of the three-day tutorial will be to assist students in performing well in the assigned coursework. Each Tuesday and Thursday morning session will be devoted to special incentives and study to enhance the student's overall social academic ability. Some of the topics for these sessions include:

1. Study skills.
2. Motivational skills.
3. Time management.
4. Social skills.
5. Communication skills.
6. Test-taking skills.
7. Media skills.
8. Values and goal setting.
9. Career planning.

Contact Person
Dr. Willie Foster
Atlanta Public Schools
210 Pryor Street, SW
Atlanta, GA 30335
404-761-5411

●────── ● ────── ●

TITLE OF PROGRAM/Business- and Community-Related
Portland Leaders' Roundtable (Oregon)

Level   (Ages 0 to 21)

Description
The Portland Investment is the ten-year plan developed by the Roundtable that includes programs for children ages 0 to 21.

Information from article: "Portland Invests in Jobs for High-risk Youth," *The Skanner*, June 25, 1986. The Portland Leaders Roundtable began in 1984 as a partnership between school, government, business, and human service agencies working together to meet high-risk youth's unemployment problems. The roundtable received a $55,000 planning grant from the Edna McConnel Clark Foundation of New York to develop a long-range comprehensive system combating the complex unemployment problems. The result will be a first-of-its-kind, comprehensive birth-to-age-21 education, training, and employment system to overcome youth employment barriers.

Goals of the master plan, called "The Portland Investment," are to reduce the number of school dropouts, help high-risk (disadvantaged youth and racial minorities) youth develop good job skills, and find jobs for them.

Barriers to employment have been identified and range from poverty, low self-esteem, and racial bias to substance abuse, young parenting, criminal records, and employer bias. Teachers, counselors, youth workers, and others formed age-level work groups to see that from preschool days to the day students leave school, there will be a recommended alternative for help.

A system of education and training for youth that:

- Attends to the needs of families and children so children have the best possible start in school

- Delivers the basic academic skills and work maturity that youth needs to be employable

- Establishes linkages among agencies and schools to meet the developmental needs of children and youth

- Consciously works to overcome two major barriers — lack of jobs and racial bias

- Provides changes within the school system to meet the individual learning needs of children and youth and to prevent school dropouts

- Develops a comprehensive system of services for out-of-school youth that merges three essential components — personal support services, education, and employment and training programs

- Improves the job climate for youth

- Provides and expands work experience opportunities for in-school and out-of-school youth

- Provides education and training programs that prepare youth to adapt to technological changes in the workplace.

Contact Person
Alcena Boozer, Frank McNamara,
   or Kathy Hostager
Portland Public Schools
P.O. Box 3107
Portland, OR 97208
503-249-2000

● ———— ● ———— ●

TITLE OF PROGRAM/Business- and Community-Related
Twelve Together Program (Michigan)

Level (High School)

Description
    This is a community-based program through the Metropolitan Detroit Youth Foundation; trains community volunteers to work with 12 children individually, for all needs.
    This high-school dropout prevention program began in 1982. Each trained peer group advisor works with 12 ninth-grade students for one year. Groups meet 30 times. The first session is a weekend retreat, followed by a parents' reception at which students make presentations from the weekend activities. Twenty-two peer group counseling sessions, along with six monthly sessions involving four groups together which are academic forums, are the main meetings. The project ends with a June Twelve Together graduation.
    The project began with 10 such support groups. About 220 to 240 students each year participate. Advisors are from the community, parents, and teachers. Businesses have also begun adopting groups, and often have them meet at the business location. Evaluation after the third year of operation showed a 17 percent higher promotion rate for student

participants as compared to a control group. Over 900 students so far have been involved.

The program applies the tenets of Weight Watchers and Alcoholics Anonymous: group commitment, confidential support meetings, promises to change self-destructive habits. The idea is that dropouts need to face underlying problems before they can change their behavior.

Twelve Together members "develop a camaraderie that makes them stick together."

Guides have been prepared for students, parents, volunteer advisors, and program planners, along with a videotape on Twelve Together.

Contact Person
Joe Radelet or Donna Lovette
Metropolitan Detroit Youth Foundation
11000 West McNichols, Suite 222
Detroit, MI 48221
313-863-9394

•————— • ————— •

TITLE OF PROGRAM/Business- and Community-Related
CCP Citizenship Competencies Program (Virginia)

Level (Adults)

Description
The Citizenship Competencies Program, approved by the Immigration and Naturalization Service (INS), is a self-contained, multi-media curriculum for teaching American history, government, and citizenship, based on the Federal Citizenship Texts and Workbooks. Available at reproduction and handling costs, it is a good option for amnesty education, naturalization preparation, and general civics instruction.

The cost for setting up a full program, including instructional materials, computers, software, and video equipment, ranges from $1,400 to $10,000, depending on the equipment ordered.

The ingredients of the program include:

1. The Citizenship Competencies Program breaks down the three Federal Citizenship texts into four levels: (1) U.S. History to the Civil War; (2) U.S. History from the Civil War; (3) Governing Our Nation; and (4) Citizenship Education.

2. These "levels," composed of smaller "units," are each subdivided into three, bite-sized, competency-based "lessons" which can be easily mastered in a single learning session.

3. The Citizenship Competencies Program Implementation Package includes 14 Curriculum Binders, a Mastery Test binder (diagnostic and prescriptive mastery tests for each unit and level and a global mastery test), a Lesson Assignment Binder with Apple IIe software, a Product Handbook containing user information and tips, and 200 CCP Plan and Profile forms for tracking individual learner progress.

4. Available multi-media options include: Print Supplements, Audio Cassette Supplements, and Voice-Interactive Courseware Supplements.

Contact Person

Andreas Achilla, Special Projects
    Team Coordinator
U.S. Basics
1700 Diagonal Road, Suite 400
Alexandria, VA 22314
703-684-1265

●————— ● ————— ●

TITLE OF PROGRAM/Business- and Community-Related
School-Community Partnerships (Colorado)

Level (Elementary, Middle School, and High School)

Description

The concept of community involvement fostered by partnerships has a number of advantages for working with at-risk students. Partnerships enable the school and community to tap a variety of resources, including senior citizens and business leaders, to provide tutoring, special activities, financial support, job training, after-school and summer jobs, mentors, incentives, and enrichment experiences for at-risk students.

Partnerships need to be built around the nature and makeup of the community. While there is no one right model, several examples currently exist in our community and schools.

Adopt-a-School: Public Service Company and Crawford Elementary were the first to develop this arrangement. Public Service provides 23 volunteers who spend approximately an hour per person per week of the official working day tutoring students at Crawford. The company has also provided supplies and supported the school thrust of personal and school pride.

Lowry Air Force Base and Park Lane Elementary have a similar arrangement and the Mountain Bell East Community Action Team provides after-school and summer enrichment programs for students at Paris, Boston, Jamaica, and Fulton Elementary Schools.

Enrichment Opportunities: Twenty-one area businesses, including United Bank of Aurora, supported the "Arts Unlimited—Positively You Week" at West Middle School. Their donations of money, supplies, and time enable 550 students to interact with musicians, craftsmen, and artists and to produce their own creative products. In the fall of 1988, Colorado National Bank sponsored a class at Columbia Middle School which focused on the banking process, handling of money, and financial planning. The class was aimed at helping eighth-grade students develop an understanding of money issues.

Many local businesses work with schools to provide incentives in the form of coupons, discounts, admission to local events, book covers, and other types of supplies. Local service groups such as Kiwanis, Lions, and

Rotary also provide scholarships for at-risk students for summer programs, medical services, and financial support for clothing, shoes, school supplies, and enrichment experiences for needy students.

In the summer of 1988, goals included recruiting partners for specific programs and establishing a mentor program.

Partnerships can also be one-on-one relationships developed between an interested volunteer and an identified student. The goal of a partnership program is to match interested volunteers, community groups, and businesses with students and schools in order to provide services unavailable as part of the regular program. Parents are key adult role models for at-risk students.

Contact Person
Debbie Lynch
Aurora Education Foundation
1085 Peoria
Aurora, CO 80011
303-344-8060, ext. 365

● ———— ● ———— ●

Bibliography

"A Population at Risk: Potential Consequences of Tougher School Standards for Student Dropouts," *American Journal of Education* 94 (February 1986): 135-181.

Bachman, J. G., S. Green, and I. D. Wirtanen, "Youth in Transition," *Dropping Out—Problem or Symptom?*, vol. 3, Institute for Social Research, University of Michigan, Ann Arbor, Michigan, 1971.

Bechard, Sue, "The Alternative School as a Dropout Prevention Strategy: A Follow-Up Study," Unpublished dissertation, University of Colorado, 1988.

Berquist, C. C., and S. E. Kruppenback, "Tracking the Elusive Dropout: A Cohort Study of Dropout Rates in a Rural School District," Paper presented at the Annual Meeting of the American Education Research Association, Washington, D.C., 1987.

Beyond Language: Social and Cultural Factors in Schooling Language Minority Students. Bilingual Education Office, State Department of Education, California State University, Los Angeles, California, 1986.

Bronfenbrenner, Urie, "Alienation and the Four Worlds of Childhood," *Phi Delta Kappan*, February 1986.

Brophy, Jere E., "Synthesis of Research on Strategies for Motivating Students to Learn," *Educational Leadership*, October 1987.

Brown, L. H., "Dropping Out: From Prediction to Prevention—A Four Year Study of High School Students from Fall 1983 through Fall 1987," Paper presented at the Annual Meeting of the American Educational Research Association, New Orleans, Louisiana, 1988.

California Curriculum News Report, "Checklist for Identifying Potential Dropouts," *California Curriculum News Report*, October 1986.

California State Department of Education, "The Problem/Scope of High Risk Youth." High Risk Youth Liaison and Field Services Unit, January 1986.

Catterall, James S., "On the Social Costs of Dropping Out of School." Stanford Education Policy Institute, December 1985.

Cuban, Larry, "The 'At-Risk' Label and the Problem of Urban School Reform," *Phi Delta Kappan*, June 1989.

"Dropout Identification Survey." Oakland County Schools, Pontiac, Michigan, May 1985.

Dropout Prevention: A Manual for Developing Comprehensive Plans. Florida Department of Education and the Florida Center for Dropout Prevention, University of Miami, September 1986.

"Early Identification of Potential Dropouts," *Programs and Practices for Students at Risk*, Dade County Public Schools, Miami, Florida, 1987.

"Early Intervention Referral Form." State Department of Public Instruction, Raleigh, North Carolina, 1985.

Education Week (May 14, 1986): 30.

Ekstrom, Ruth B., Margaret Goertz, Judith Pollack, and Donald Rock, "Who Drops Out of High School and Why? Findings from a National Study," *Teachers College Record* 87 (Spring 1986): 356-373.

Enda, Jodi, "Hispanic Poverty: Our Growing Crisis," *Rocky Mountain News*, Denver, Colorado, December 1986.

Fine, Michelle, "Why Urban Adolescents Drop Into and Out of Public High School," *Teachers College Record* 87 (Spring 1986): 393-409.

Hahn, Andrew, "Reaching Out to America's Dropouts: What to Do?," *Phi Delta Kappan*, December 1987.

Hamby, John V., "How to Get an 'A' on Your Dropout Prevention Report Card," *Education Leadership*, February 1989.

Hammack, Floyd Morgan, "Large School Systems' Dropout Reports: An Analysis of Definitions, Procedures, and Findings," *Teachers College Record* 87 (Spring 1986): 324-341.

The High School Dropout Problem: Strategies for Reduction. High School Dropout Prevent Prevention Network of Southeast Michigan, Wayne State University, June 1985.

"The Human Factor: A Key to Excellence in Education." National Association of Social Workers, 1985.

LAUSD Dropout Prevention/Recovery Committee, "A Study of Student Dropout in the Los Angeles Unified School District," Summary presented to Dr. Harry Handler, Superintendent, and the Board of Education, Los Angeles, California, 1985.

Lehr, Judy Brown, and Hazel Wiggins Harris, *At-Risk, Low-Achieving Students in the Classroom.* National Education Association, Washington, D.C., 1988.

Levin, Henry M., *The Costs to the Nation of Inadequate Education.* Study prepared for the Select Committee on Equal Education Opportunity, U.S. Senate. U.S. Government Printing Office, Washington, D.C., 1972.

Los Angeles County Office of Education, *The Prevention of Truancy: Programs and Strategies That Address Problems of Truancy and Dropouts.* 1985.

McDill, Edward L., Gary Natriello, and Aaron M. Pallas, "Raising Standards and Retaining Students: The Impact of the Reform Recommendations on Potential Dropouts," *Review of Educational Research* 55 (Winter 1985): 415-433.

Mizell, M. Hayes, *First Steps: Considerations Preliminary to the Development of Dropout Prevention Policies and Programs.* Youth Employment Coordinating Council, Columbia, South Carolina, August 1986.

National Commission on Excellence in Education, *A Nation at Risk.* U.S. Government Printing Office, Washington, D.C., 1983.

Networking for Solutions: For Dropout Prevention. Center for Dropout Prevention, University of Miami, Miami, Florida, 1986.

Operation Rescue: A Blueprint for Success. National Foundation for the Imaprovement of Education, 1986.

Orr, Margaret Terry, *Keeping Students in School.* Jossey-Bass Publishers, San Francisco, California, 1987.

Orum, L. S., *The Education of Hispanics: Status and Implications*. National Council of La Raza, Washington, D.C., 1986.

Orum, L. S., *Hispanic Dropouts: Community Responses*. Office of Research, Advocacy and Legislation, National Council of La Raza, Washington, D.C., July 1984.

Pasternak, Cindy S., *Why Isn't Johnny in School? Effective Strategies for Attendance Improvement and Truancy Prevention*. Tri-County Dropout Prevention Program, Grundy-Kendall Educational Service Region, Illinois, September 1986.

Peng, S. S., and R. T. Takai, *High School Dropouts: Descriptive Information from High School and Beyond*. National Center for Education Statistics, Washington, D.C., 1983.

Phelan, William T., and Joyce Taylor-Gibson, "Obstacles to High School Graduation: The Case of Hispanics," Paper presented at convention of the American Education Research Association in San Francisco, April 1986.

Reconnecting Youth: The Next Stage of Reform. Report from the Business Advisory Commission of the Education Commission of the States. Education Commission of the States, Denver, Colorado, October 1985.

Rodriquez, Victor E., *Student Dropouts: A Look at the Issues*. Southwest Regional Laboratory, California, 1985.

Rumberger, Russell W., "Dropping Out of High School: The Influence of Race, Sex, and Family Background," *American Educational Research Journal* 20 (Summer 1983).

Rumberger, Russell W., *High School Dropouts: A Problem for Research, Policy, and Practices*. Stanford University, Stanford, California, September 1986.

San Diego City Schools Planning, Research, and Evaluation Division, "The 1982-83 School Leaver Study of the San Diego Unified School District." Prepared by Robert B. Barr, consultant for the Planning, Research and Evaluation Division of the Research Department, San Diego, California, 1985.

School Dropouts: Everybody's Problem. Institute for Educational Leadership, Washington, D.C., May 1986.

"Schools, Treatment of Pupils Said to Boost Dropout Rate," *Education Week*, Febrary 1985.

Steinberg, Lawrence, Patricia Lin Blinde, and Kenyon S. Chan, *Dropping Out among Language Minority Youth: A Review of the Literature*. National Center for Bilingual Research, Los Alamitos, California, June 1982.

Stern, David, "Dropout Prevention and Recovery in California." University of California, Berkeley, California, 1986 (mimeo).

Task Force on Education for Economic Growth, *Action for Excellence*. Education Commission of the States, Denver, Colorado, 1983.

U.S. Census Bureau, *Statistical Abstract of the United States, 1985*. 106th ed., U.S. Government Printing Office, Washington, D.C., 1986.

U.S. Department of Education, *Effective Compensatory Education Sourcebook, Volume I: A Review of Effective Educational Practices*. 1986.

Weber, James, "Vocational Education and Its Role in Dropout Reduction," *Facts and Findings*, National Center for Research in Vocational Education, Spring 1986.

Weber, J. M., and C. Silvani-Lacey, *Building Basic Skills: The Dropout*. The National Center for Research in Vocational Education, Ohio State University, Columbus, Ohio, 1983.

Wehlage, Gary G., and Robert A. Rutter, "Dropping Out: How Much Do Schools Contribute to the Problem," *Teachers College Record* 87 (Spring 1986): 374-392.

Wehlage, Gary G., Robert A. Rutter, and Anne Turnbaugh, "A Program Model for At-Risk High School Students," *Educational Leadership*, March 1987.

Weikart, David P., John R. Berrueta-Clement, Lawrence J. Schweinhart, W. Steven Barnett, and Ann S. Epstein, *Changed Lives: The Effects of Perry Preschool Program on Youths through Age 19*. High/Scope Educational Research Foundation, 1984.

Wells, Shirley, Sue Bechard, and John V. Hamby, "How to Identify At-Risk Students," *Solutions and Strategies*, National Dropout Prevention Center, Clemson University, Clemson, South Carolina, July 1989.

William T. Grant Foundation Commission on Work, Family and Citizenship, "The Forgotten Half: Pathways to Success for America's Youth and Young Families," *Phi Delta Kappan*, December 1988.

Wisconsin Vocational Studies Center, *Staying In: A Dropout Prevention Handbook K-12*. University of Wisconsin, Madison, Wisconsin, 1981.

Grade Level Index

Locality Index

Subject Index